~NEW YOI
ONTARIO
&WESTERN
IN THE
DIESEL AGE

ROBERT E. MOHOWSKI
WITH ARTWORK BY CARL A. OHLSON

For my parents, Jennie and Edward S. Mohowski

ANDOVER
JUNCTION
PUBLICATIONS
P.O. BOX 1160   ANDOVER, NJ 07821

"We must be satisfied with shadows and outlines because the irremediable incompleteness of the historical record reminds us of how every historian is compelled to create the past out of the pieces that survive."

—Drew Gilpin Faust,
New York Times Book Review,
Nov. 17, 1991

PUBLISHING DIRECTOR
Joyce C. Mooney

PUBLISHER
Stephen A. Esposito

EDITORIAL & ART DIRECTOR
Mike Schafer

SPECIAL ASSISTANCE
Rick Johnson   Mark Llanuza

(COVER ILLUSTRATION) Through trains on O&W's Northern Division were infrequent north of Randallsville and, prior to 1948, road diesels were usually confined to the Southern and Scranton divisions. During the evening prior to this scene, young Sam Reeder of Munnsville, N.Y., heard the sound of an unfamiliar horn and locomotive passing north along the ridge above town. Neglecting his Saturday morning chores the next day, he walked up the hill from the village in hopes of seeing the new locomotive on its return run. He got a double surprise.

Northbound GE 44-ton switcher 105, returning to its assigned post at Fulton, N.Y., was sitting at the depot awaiting the southbound through freight. Within minutes, the crew of a gray-and-yellow "streamliner," rather than the familiar 2-8-0, gave a short acknowledgement to the familiar boy at Munnsville as it rolled south to its connection with train US-2 at Norwich. Company officials had already made the decision to repaint the five 44-tonners in the new gray-and-yellow scheme of the new FT's, so such colorful meets were soon to become rare memories—certainly worth a scolding upon returning home.

Artist Carl Ohlson recreated the scene in water colors and pen and ink. Models, archive photographs and numerous photos made during several visits to the recently restored Munnsville depot were carefully studied beforehand. John Taibi, the depot's resourceful and dedicated owner, is a good friend of both the artist and the author. Across-the-tracks neighbor Sam Reeder is an avid O&W historian, and all four spend occasional weekends at the station in a hearty fellowship of conversation and laughter.

(TITLE PAGE): Northbound symbol freight BC-3 takes to the air at Ferndale, N.Y., on March 23, 1957. The A-B set of O&W Electro-Motive FT's symbolize the railroad's big step into dieselization. Although the FT's were not the first diesels acquired by O&W, they were the first road diesels, purchased specifically for the goal of complete dieselization. The goal was achieved in 1948, nine years before this memorable view was recorded during the last week of O&W operation in March 1957.—JIM SHAUGHNESSY.

(THIS PAGE) Two O&W crew members proudly pose with their FT for the camera of fellow employee, Guy Twaddell, at New Haven's Maybrook Yard circa 1950.—GUY TWADDELL, O&W SOCIETY COLLECTION.

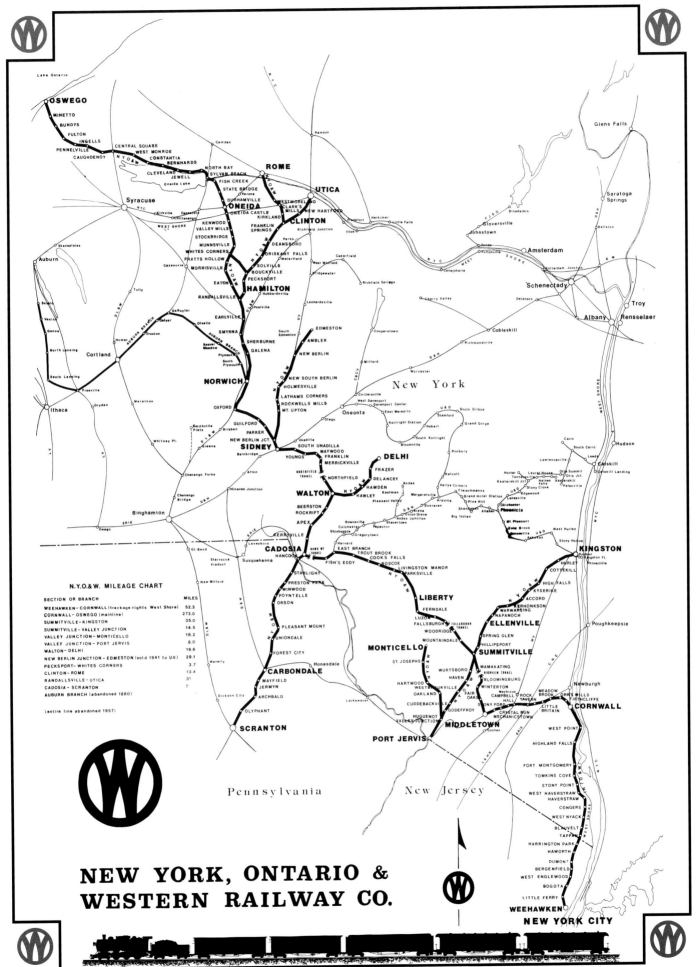

N.Y.O.&W. MILEAGE CHART

SECTION OR BRANCH	MILES
WEEHAWKEN – CORNWALL (trackage rights West Shore)	52.3
CORNWALL – OSWEGO (mainline)	273.0
SUMMITVILLE – KINGSTON	35.0
SUMMITVILLE – VALLEY JUNCTION	14.5
VALLEY JUNCTION – MONTICELLO	16.2
VALLEY JUNCTION – PORT JERVIS	8.0
WALTON – DELHI	16.6
NEW BERLIN JUNCTION – EDMESTON (sold 1941 to U.V.)	29.1
PECKSPORT – WHITES CORNERS	3.7
CLINTON – ROME	13.4
RANDALLSVILLE – UTICA	3*
CADOSIA – SCRANTON	5*
AUBURN BRANCH (abandoned 1880)	

(entire line abandoned 1957)

NEW YORK, ONTARIO & WESTERN RAILWAY CO.

Map courtesy O&W Historical Society

Foreword

In 1945 my parents moved to Teaneck, N.J., a few blocks from New York Central's West Shore Line. I joined them the following year upon returning from military service. With a new Kodak Medalist, I started shooting K-11 Pacifics and L-2 and L-3 Mohawks on the West Shore. It didn't take long for me to discover the schedules of NYO&W passenger trains, powered by its 4-8-2's, which also used NYC tracks between Cornwall, N.Y., and Weehawken, N.J. O&W trains had distinctive high-mounted headlights which showed quickly as they crested the Teaneck grade and came toward me at West Englewood. A rarer treat was to see an occasional O&W freight with a 450-series heavy Mountain type. On even rarer occasions, it was double-headed with a 300-series 2-8-0.

In June 1946, the late Ed Hansen, the Railroad Enthusiasts' trip chairman, arranged a fan trip on the NYO&W from Weehawken to Walton, N.Y. The fare was ridiculously low, and the weather was perfect. On the head end was

Mountain-type 405, which had previously graced the *Mountaineer Limited*. The Otto Kuhler stream styling and maroon paint of pre-war days had disappeared, and the 405 was in standard steam locomotive black. A coach-observation car brought up the rear.

Arriving Middletown we could see it was still a busy railroad center. A large wooden coaling tower and a roundhouse served a stable of steam power, and the yard tracks were loaded with freight cars and wooden cars of O&W's passenger fleet. As the train passed the engine terminal, I snapped a set of O&W's new FT sets. Just beyond the shops were engine storage tracks loaded with dead O&W steam power: Camelback Moguls, Ten-Wheelers and switchers, Class P and W Consolidations and even a rare "Bull Moose" 2-10-2, the 351. Near Liberty, N.Y., our train stopped to meet a southbound through job led by an A-B-B-A FT set. We passed through Roscoe, N.Y., where the well-preserved body of an early Sykes railbus, the 801, rested quietly.

Subsequent trips to the NYO&W by car with Johnny Krause, Harry Zannie, Ted Gay and Sherman Dance took me to previously unexplored areas of the road. Sherman and I even rode the former branch to Edmeston, N.Y., which had become a part of the Unadilla Valley, on the pilot of No. 200, a GE 70-tonner. I recall seeing the O&W herald built into an old railroad structure at Edmeston.

The FT's were soon joined by the by the 500- and 820-series F3's. A fleet of NW2 switchers completed the modernization by joining the earlier group of five GE 44-tonners which had lost their earlier maroon and black and now matched the EMDs in gray and yellow.

The O&W's passenger runs along the West Shore were the first diesel-powered trains in regular service on that route. Summer camp specials often used FT A&B sets which usually were considered freight locomotives. It wasn't long before those diesels were also handling O&W freights on the West Shore.

In 1951 I received permission to ride the cab of the daily passenger train from Weehawken to Roscoe and back, the service to Walton having been cut back since the RRE fan trip. The train had a single A unit, a heater car, an RPO and several borrowed NYC coaches. The run through the long Bergen Hill Tunnel from Weehawken and up the West Shore's well-maintained right-of-way was smooth and steady. After the stop at Cornwall, we entered onto NYO&W's own iron. Most of the double track was gone, and the bridges presented a strange sight with half of their structure removed. The ride was no longer as smooth as it had been, and one wondered if the curves weren't really a series of tangents at slight angles to each other. The train nevertheless maintained a creditable speed.

One could see that Middletown could still lay claim to being a real railroad town because the shops were still active. Passengers got off at such stations as Ferndale, Liberty, Livingston Manor and, finally, Roscoe, the end of the run where the body of the 801 was still a landmark.

F3 501 was turned on the wye and after the crew had lunch, we began our southbound trip. At Middletown we had an engine and crew change. The new crew continued to Weehawken with engine 503, stayed overnight and repeated the run to Roscoe and back to Middletown the following day.

There are some who say the New York, Ontario & Western was a road that wasn't needed and should never have been built. Nevertheless

it moved millions of tons of freight during its lifetime, which included war material during two major conflicts. It brought inhabitants along its route closer to big city life and made possible the creation of the Catskill hotel business. As a result, summer passenger traffic boomed and required a motley assortment of wooden O&W cars and additional cars leased from NYC, Reading, Jersey Central and Florida East Coast among others. Each year the railroad issued a thick catalog listing the resort hotels such as Grossingers, the Nevele, Sunrise, Concord and the Stevensville Lake Hotel. The attractions were food, water sports and night life. Many famous entertainers such as Mollie Icon, Myron Cohen, Belle Baker, Dan Tannen and Buddy Hackett got their start or worked the area in their early days. Many hotels served a Jewish clientele and observed dietary laws and offered special High Holy Day services featuring world-famous opera singers as cantors.

With improvements to New York Route 17, entrepreneurs bought old Cadillac limousines, picked up Catskill-bound riders in Brooklyn and the Bronx and delivered them directly to the doors of their hotels. On Route 17, the vintage Caddies were often seen loaded with suitcases wherever they could be secured. If not as elegant as the train, the limos offered a service at a price and convenience that the O&W just could not match, even with shiny new diesels.

Dieselization brought needed savings to the O&W and prolonged the life of the carrier for several more years. Some segments remain today, operated by Conrail as industrial spurs. NW2 switcher 116 was eventually bought by the New York, Susquehanna & Western and was repainted in its original NYO&W colors giving newer railfans a glimpse of what had been and recalling for older fans a reminder of a simpler past.

I'm delighted that the story of the diesel years of the NYO&W is being published. The story could only be told properly by someone who delved into the O&W first hand, had access to the archives and, more importantly, who met the people who *were* the NYO&W: former employees, shippers and riders. Bob Mohowski's credentials as a teacher, historian, rail enthusiast and model builder qualify him to fill a vacant niche in the lore of this fascinating carrier.

Harold Carstens
Newton, N.J.
June 1, 1992

(FACING PAGE) In the vicinity of Ridgefield Park, N.J., double-headed Camelbacks move a hopper train over West Shore's four-track territory. From Weehawken to CN tower at Cornwall, O&W trains operated under NYC rules and timetable. O&W men also had to have the current West Shore employees' timetable in their possession and be familiar to its contents while on NYC track. In addition, West Shore bulletin orders were posted in the Middletown offices so O&W crews could be kept current with daily operational situations south of Cornwall.
—GERRY BERNET COLLECTION.

Introduction

As this book goes to press, we are rapidly approaching the half-century mark since the final single-note trumpeting of a locomotive air horn cleared the rural crossings that intersected the rights-of-ways of the New York, Ontario & Western Railway. Indeed, it is has become difficult to even find those pathways as both development and nature claim the transportation corridors that were the routes of the NYO&W ("O&W" to its friends).

However, those years have failed to quell an enthusiastic desire for knowledge of matters O&W within the ranks of railroad historians. Each newly discovered O&W photograph, corporate record, operational file, switch key, lantern or timetable continues to be lovingly and carefully examined, shared and discussed with like-minded comrades. Every shred of company paper is analyzed for whatever bit of insight and understanding it may offer to the forever incomplete mosaic of the road's history.

More in its passing than during its lifetime, the O&W gave rise to a unique camaraderie among the people who have made something more than a hobby of examining its fascinating personality and physical remnants. This society of O&W aficionados shares strong friendships and devotions to their formal organizations. They refer to the road in the present tense and speak of visits to Cadosia, Northfield Tunnel or Lyon Brook Trestle in the same manner as others visit Horseshoe Curve or Cajon Pass. Some have taken it much further. To spend an evening with depot owner John Taibi in the restored Munnsville, N.Y., O&W station in an atmosphere of kerosene lantern fumes and clicking telegraph keys is to confirm the O&W's existence. The acknowledgments in this volume are a partial listing of that unique and special family of which I am honored to be a member, and our insatiable desire for more information on "our" railroad gave rise to this book.

I believe that, to understand the events of a more recent era, it is necessary to have some concept of what had occurred earlier. Therefore, we start with a general history of the NYO&W.

I maintain that O&W history has been both carelessly disparaged on one hand and raised to a level of mysticism on the other. A simplistic view sees the road's entire history in terms of its last two decades and takes the line's efforts to stay alive during the period of bankruptcy for its larger story. The resulting impression from this perspective is that the line never made money nor made any significant contribution to the transportation needs or growth of its region, state or nation. But if that were so, I have to wonder why a federal court and so many individuals on all levels of government, business and industry spent the greater part of twenty years attempting to reorganize the company.

We are separated from the past by a wall of time and a higher and wider barrier of contemporary values that shadows every aspect of our existence. Great care should be taken in making judgments after the facts, and no judgments should be made using solely a framework of contemporary values for determining past successes and failures. It is unreasonable to condemn the planners of the New York & Oswego Midland— O&W's predecessor—for not anticipating the transportation requirements of the second half of the 20th Century. Their concern was with immediate necessity and opportunity. It was a thinking that was consistent with the relatively unrestrained capitalistic climate of the period, for the OM did not suddenly appear as an entity out of nowhere. It came out of thought, institutions and debates—the dynamic totality of forces that define every period of history.

On the other hand are those who romanticize the railroad's history, becoming misty-eyed at the sight of the initials N.Y.O.&W. and do not care to understand or look beyond their photo or hardware collection. Although I, too, confess to some sort of emotional attachment to the road, I cannot be satisfied with either stand and must continue to indulge a profound curiosity that would like to know every detail of this transportation company that no longer exists.

An individual of particular importance in the events leading up to O&W's dieselization was Frederic E. Lyford, the railroad's first trustee. It was Lyford, more than any other individual, who made the decision to convert to diesel power. Even before I had the opportunity to know him through his family's remembrances, he came through all those brittle, dusty papers as a man of integrity and sound judgment. Entrusted with the O&W's limited resources, he carefully balanced expenditure against the needed productivity that diesels could provide, taking into account all the facets of the problem ranging from the impact diesels would have on employees (many would be furloughed) to their effect on track and roadbed.

His daughter, Nancy Lyford, and her sister and brothers, daughter and son-in-law graciously provided background on her father and took great interest in this effort and provided steady encouragement.

EVERY STEAM-ERA RAILROAD lost a good deal of its individuality with the arrival of its first diesels. Think about it. At quick glance, only a coat of paint told you if you were looking at an O&W diesel or one from a neighboring road. This loss of individuality became even more apparent when mainline road diesels, purchased by the hundreds, showed that railroads had much more in mind than simply toying with small oil-fueled yard units. Fortunately, a curious and diligent few soon noted that it *was* more than paint that made the diesels different. Later, increasing sophistication among the writers and editors of the "rail hobby" magazines, particularly *Extra 2200 South*, The Locomotive News Magazine, encouraged careful study and documentation of internal-combustion motive power.

The story of O&W's diesels is not a complex one, and—more so than was the case with the road's steam locomotives—much diesel information is generic and can be gathered from a greater number of sources. A roster of 40 locomotives, representing but four models, makes the road one of the smaller Class I carriers of its day. None of the four models could be considered rare for their time, nor were they equipped with features that made them especially unique (except for that paint, of course). The occasional suggestion that the road was the first in the U.S. to dieselize is not true, and the architecture of O&W stations and the appearance of its steam locomotives—to name just two examples—were more important in establishing the O&W's character.

Yet, the diesels are worth attention simply because locomotives in general—be they steam, diesel, or electric—have been and continue to be, the first focus of attention for even the most casual of train-watchers. More importantly, diesels are a highly significant part of the technological history of a nation inextricably connected to railroads. Thus, diesels are an integral part of the O&W story and, in the case of this particular railroad, made that story longer by several years.

The O&W went to complete diesel operation earlier than most of its neighbors. In truth, the road had little choice in the matter since it simply could not afford continued steam operations. At the end of 1949, there were almost 11,000 diesels in service in the U.S. On a national scale, these diesels handled almost 35 percent of total freight gross ton-miles, almost 50 percent of the total passenger-train miles and almost 50 percent of yard-locomotive hours for the year. At the time, O&W had been dieselized for more than a year and was well ahead of these national figures and had been for some time.

(FACING PAGE) O&W F-units 807 and 502 get a respite from their daily labors at Middletown shops. A few days after this March 23, 1957, date, they would get an even longer rest. A shopman, having heard of the intended shutdown of the entire railroad, faces a future that will call for some crucial decisions.—JIM SHAUGHNESSY.

In tracing the development of each of the four diesel models that were used by the O&W, I hope to provide readers with greater detail on a few topics that had puzzled me and other rail historians for some time, such as the functioning of dynamic brakes and manual transition. To the best of my knowledge, nothing in the rail history press to date has provided anything more than a simple paragraph explaining just what made dynamic braking possible.

It was my good fortune to have ridden in FT's and F3's on several roads when these units were still fairly common. I plied my enginemen hosts with plenty of questions about the operation of the units. One experience came to mind while pondering the intricacies of dynamic braking being covered in this book: One night in the early 1960's, I was aboard Erie Lackawanna freight NY-99. We had just cleared the roaring blackness of Otisville Tunnel and were beginning the 14-mile grade down the Shawangunk Ridge into Port Jervis, N.Y. Except for a few gauge lights, the cab of the FT was dark and relatively quiet. The engineer was manipulating levers on the control stand when, from an electrical cabinet somewhere behind me, came a couple of loud slams and flashes of light that escaped between cracks. Upon regaining my seat, I asked what the commotion was about. The engineer shifted his cigar and replied that he was "Putting 'em in dynamics . . ." I now know that it was the shift of large electrical contactors from "motor" to "dynamic" modes that caused the unexpected noise and arcing that I had witnessed.

I was surprised not to find a definitive history of Electro-Motive, the builder of all but five O&W diesels. This company is one of the world's premier diesel-locomotive manufacturers. Two small company-sponsored books, On Time and The Dilworth Story, offer limited background in company-approved texts. Likewise, there was little published material on the development of the F3 or NW2 locomotives. Trade publications such as *Railway Age, Railway Mechanical Engineer* and the Locomotive Cyclopedia as well as *Extra 2200 South* provided much of the information on these two diesel models.

The railroad churned out a great deal of paperwork in the form of studies, reports and applications concerning the change to diesel power. Although I found and studied many of these documents, there were specific references to others that I could not find. Further, statistics compiled for each of the three diesel purchases frequently were at odds for that particular purchase. I selected what appeared to be the final figures but caution readers concerned with absolute accuracy to do their own checking.

I have relied heavily on the two dozen volumes that documented the railroad's bankruptcy proceedings for much of the information contained herein. Mr. Bill Drake kindly loaned me

his personal set, and I also made use of a set that resides in the archives of the O&W Chapter-National Railway Historical Society.

The Reconstruction Finance Corporation played a large role in providing the needed financing for many railroads to acquire diesels, pay taxes and meet other monetary obligations during the Depression and World War II. Roger Cook, a good friend and knowledgeable in matters of business finance, provided information on this federal agency that aided the O&W.

The fun source of O&W information for this book was the road's employees. In the early 1960's, I learned of the annual O&W Veterans' Picnic held at Firemen's Park in Hancock, N.Y. There I met Elwin Mumford, Oscar and Guy Bennett, Bill Fleming, Fred Beck, Fred Lewis, Ted Lewis, Lou Crawford, Benny Stevens, John Fife, George Bensing and many other O&W folks who filled my mind with stories, facts, names and places that contributed to the O&W legend.

These people did not regard themselves as heroes or unique individuals, but they knew they were part of a colorful story and heritage which they were eager to pass down. Many of them became good friends with whom I corresponded and visited. Elwin Mumford, Fred Lewis and Fred Beck became particularly close friends, and they took me to places of memorable occurrences in their railroad lives, providing depth and feeling that could be added to the photos, movies, paper and hardware that were the physical remnants of the abandoned system.

It was a particular challenge to find the color photographs contained herein. One reason lies in the very criticism that was leveled at the railroad for building a route through the rural sections of New York State—scant population. There simply were not enough people living along the route who had an interest in, or cared to indulge in, color photography, and many could probably not afford to do so anyway. The O&W was not running many trains during the period that color photography became popular, and it took a singleness of purpose to find and shoot those that were on the line. Remember, too, that the convenient highway system we have today that makes distant places so accessible was still in its infancy. As for the O&W itself serving as a means of transportation for photographers, its passenger service was limited in both distance and frequency and ended altogether in 1953.

We also need to put O&W's diesel era in perspective. With the incredible interest in diesels today, it is hard for some of us to realize that, during post-World War II years, diesels were of secondary interest to the relatively few active enthusiasts of the period. The remaining steam operations in the Northeast were a powerful attraction, and few photographers chose to ignore them in favor of diesel searches.

Several people, without whose help this book

would have been very lean, have already been mentioned and here are others who allowed me to write more confidently on a few subjects: Pete Rasmussen and Pete Brill of the Middletown & New Jersey, that amazing century-old remnant of the Oswego Midland/New Jersey Midland operation, explained the of intricacies and idiosyncrasies of 44-tonners; Don Hogle of the Salt Lake, Garfield & Western did likewise, in addition to allowing me to ride his ex-O&W 44-tonner on the little road that parallels the former Western Pacific main line out of Salt Lake City; Jack Wheelihan and Bill Gardner of EMD proofed the manuscript and offered suggestions for improvement; Preston Cook, himself an author as well as a former EMD employee, also reviewed the material; Randy Brown, a person of wide interests and intellect, suggested information sources and interpreted electrical mysteries; Richard Jahn of the Anthracite Roads Historical Society—who with the group has restored several F3's to operation—not only added information to the F3 chapter, but also provided a detailed tour of the mechanical and electrical innards of those beautifully restored units.

Other recognitions are in order. Marv Cohen made the production of this volume much easier than I expected. Marv is a quiet, unassuming person, but a wonderful source of regional railroad information and photos (the largest color part of this book). Dan Myers and his family had a close relationship with the railroad, and he offered many suggestions and pieces of information. Richard Howe, whose father was a station agent, answered frequent questions about a number of details, and Dr. James W. Darlington of Brandon University kindly allowed me to use some of his maps. Joe Bux, Doug Ellison, Mike Holdridge and Bill Scott either loaned material or pointed me toward sources, and Richard Taylor, Lou Boselli and Rusty Recordon proofread all material. Mrs. David Connor kindly permitted the use of her late husband's excellent collection of O&W slides, and Mr. Chet Stietz loaned some pictures from the Harry Zannie collection. Long-time friends Mike Bednar, Ken Bealer, Don Wallworth and Bob Collins provided several photographs from their extensive collections.

Hal Carstens has been a close friend, and we have shared our O&W interest on many occasions. Because of his first-hand experiences with the road, he was a primary source of information. He constantly reminds me—in good humor, I trust—that he rode and photographed the railroad directly while I can only vicariously experience the O&W from his movies and prints. I thought it appropriate for his foreword to set the stage for the following work.

I appreciate the review attention, from the professional perspective, given to my efforts by four individuals. Wallace Abbey, who is researching Santa Fe's FT fleet, reviewed my findings on that model and added a few new pieces of information. John F. Kirkland's employment and research in the diesel industry has made him an authoritative source of diesel history. He wrote extensive margin notes on my text and added interesting pieces of O&W history. The late George M. Leilich served as a division superintendent with the Lehigh Valley, general manager of the Western Maryland and staff officer with the Chessie System and the Association of American Railroads. He was quite familiar with EMD F-units and freely shared his knowledge. Walter Rich, president of Delaware Otsego Corporation, owner of the New York, Susquehanna & Western, grew up in the vicinity of the O&W and holds an avid interest in its history and loaned photographs from his collection.

The railroad's short-lived *Mountaineer Limited*, its stream-styled, summer-only passenger train, has drawn an interest totally out of proportion to both its limited existence and the length of its run. Paul Lubliner, who has taken a monastic vow of dedication to its memory and the uncov-

ering of its most minute details, provided a brief history of this train as well as its only known color photo. The degree of his resolution can be judged from the fact that he had refused to paint his model of the train until he determined the interior color of the cars' vestibules!

My good friend Carl Ohlson, with whom I've explored library and private collections, hundreds of photographs and miles of the old roadbed, was an indispensable part of this book. His dust jacket painting and artwork interspersed through the book and photographs, gives us another viewpoint of O&W history. I am honored to have such generous friends.

Library staffs at Drew and Lehigh universities provided help at their facilities and kindly suggested sources or obtained information from other collections.

Finally, my thanks to Joyce Mooney, Steve Esposito and Mike Schafer of Andover Junction who shared my enthusiasm for the project.

Robert E. Mohowski
Franklin Lakes, N.J.
Nov. 2, 1993

1/NYO&W: A History

The United States had recently survived the ultimate test of nationhood—civil war—just before the story of the O&W began. In very large measure, it was the changes wrought by that war that set the stage for a different America, one that further encouraged speculative enterprises such as that which would eventually be known as the New York, Ontario & Western Railway.

In addition to battlefield losses, the great conflict had required, used and destroyed resources at a rate that the nation had not believed possible, and replacement and rebuilding were done in equal and frequently greater scale. Such work required and developed organizational, managerial and mobilization skills that a certain breed of men would remember and apply to the nation's industrial growth in the post-Civil War era. Allan Nevins, in WAR FOR THE UNION, saw that the experience had "transformed an inchoate nation, individualistic in temper and wedded to improvisation, into a shaped and disciplined nation, increasingly aware of the importance of plan and control."

The closing decades of the 19th Century found

these industrial and former military leaders, with their new thinking and skills and their enlarged concept of scale, at the forefront of American business activity developing all manner of commercial and industrial projects. They wielded broad power and influence in both political and financial circles. They thought, planned, schemed and acted, some to the benefit of the nation and humanity and others for themselves.

The Industrial Revolution, begun in England late in the 18th Century, did not truly appear in the U.S. much before 1800. For the most part, American energies were focused on westward expansion and agriculture. Shortages of capital and labor restricted the development of manufacturing and transportation systems, but after 1840, coal-fueled furnaces, steam-powered machinery, American and European capital and immigrant labor brought the nation into the industrial age with increasing determination.

By 1850, railroads had clearly established themselves as a transportation technology of proven merit, and the Civil War had provided ample additional evidence of their superiority over other forms of transport. Even before the war, an expanding network of track had well begun reaching for resources that were as far-flung as the nation's geography. President Lincoln's signing of the Pacific Railroad Bill in 1862 had essentially put the faith—and the money—of the federal government in steam locomotion to bind the nation together from Atlantic to Pacific. It was the necessary political step that allowed future presidents to say "The United States is . . ." rather than "The United States are . . ." when speaking of national action or policy.

But there was no further plan for some sort of national and rational rail network—a plan that might have avoided the all-too-frequent and seemingly senseless duplication of routes that would occur. It was very likely that such a plan would have been impossible to implement, much less enforce, in a climate that would have had little patience with government restrictions and believed that money was to be made in any railroad enterprise.

In 1869, the telegraph message from Promontory, Utah, may have said, "Done!" but it also marked the beginning of many other rail projects. Although few were as grandiose as the efforts of the Central and Union Pacific railroads, the new projects frequently duplicated in microcosm all that was good and bad with the first transcontinental effort, including the all-important political, social and commercial unification.

In the post-Civil War half-century, which had the highest hopes attached to Manifest Destiny and unlimited industrial and commercial expansion, the railroad was seen as the vehicle that would usher in a great age of prosperity. The rural farmer, small-town merchant, big city manufacturer—and political figures at every level of government—all saw the opportunities presented by a railroad linking their location (and interests) with other communities, and they devoted their combined energies to the task of starting new lines. Meanwhile, the successful rail systems constructed before the war were expanding by merger or new construction.

AMONG THOSE REACTING to all these forces was a group of men in New York who wished to establish a new railroad across the state between the routes of the Erie Railroad on the south and the New York Central & Hudson River to the north. They believed, or were sold the belief, that Oswego, N.Y., would become the major port of the lower Great Lakes and that the port could be connected with New York City by an economical route through the mountainous regions of Sullivan, Delaware and Chenango counties. Once it was in place, they envisioned this shorter route as attracting business away from the two established lines and developing an on-line economy that would flourish at great profit to the population and the company. They called it the New York & Oswego Midland Railroad.

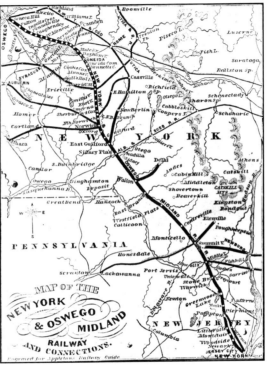

(ABOVE) In a mood of exaggerated optimism, the NY&OM appeared willing to plan a branch line at the slightest suggestion of potential profit. The southern part of the route between Middletown, N.Y., and Pompton, N.J., was never constructed, and even at this early stage in its life, the railroad displayed a "topographical artistic license" for straightening its route. —AUTHOR'S COLLECTION.

(ABOVE) In the manner that many treat automobiles today, early locomotives were not mere mechanical "things" but were regarded as objects of awe, affection and perhaps even deification. The locomotive engineer, in control of the potent forces within OM No. 55, was highly respected. Mark Twain made it clear that the same stature and dignity be afforded to river pilots of slightly earlier decades.—AUTHOR'S COLLECTION

(FACING PAGE) A stocky P-class 2-8-0 on what is probably the way freight out of Cadosia, N.Y., hustles along the Lackawanna River through Archbald, Pa., on Oct. 24, 1946. Severe flooding along here in 1942 wiped out several sections of track and forced the O&W to detour.—J. R. QUINN COLLECTION.

For several reasons, the Midland's planners chose to deviate from patterns of development that dated back to colonial times. Early America's major population and fledgling manufacturing centers needed access to water transportation, and so they developed on rivers or sheltered harbors. Canals, representing a natural progression in water transporation, generally followed rivers and streams for easier grades and a reliable water supply. The railroads also followed streams for the easier grades but also to serve those commu-

This trestle on the Auburn Branch was south of Venice, N.Y. This extension left the main line at Norwich and opened for service in July 1871. Lack of patronage caused an early discontinuance of passenger service, and freight service was sporadic. In 1879, all service was ended, parts of the line sold to another railroad and the remainder scrapped.—AUTHOR'S COLLECTION.

nities and industries that had earlier been established along the waterways. Although the Midland didn't totally ignore this picture, it put great faith in its own ability to create wholly new sources of revenue and develop an all-new Great Lakes-New York City transportation corridor.

The plans were easy to promote in a freewheeling era marked by governmental laissez-faire and a resultant attitude of caveat emptor—certainly as far as investments were concerned. A key player among the Midland's promoters was Oswego entrepreneur and Speaker of the New York State Assembly, DeWitt C. Littlejohn. He became Midland's president and, with a fine disdain for the glacier-gouged topography of New York State, boasted of building a line ". . . athwart the rivers and valleys and at right angles to the mountains." Incorporation papers were completed in 1866, construction contracts were awarded and work began in June of 1868.

To fulfill Littlejohn's prophesy, some five years were needed to put the roadbed over the many hills (tunneling through three of them), bridge the ravines and rivers and overcome a chronic shortage of construction and equipment funds. But, the NY&OM was indeed built. The cost of constructing the Middletown-Oswego main

line was $26.2 million. In view of the rugged topography the line traversed, it is not surprising that this sum was well in excess of the costs originally projected.

The Midland's own route took it as far south as Middletown, N.Y. By gaining control of the Middletown, Unionville & Water Gap and the New Jersey Midland—today's Middletown & New Jersey and the New York, Susquehanna & Western respectively—the Midland was able to reach Jersey City, N.J., at the doorstep of New York City. The result was a circuitous through route between Jersey City and Oswego with several connecting branches to reach other railroads, cities and villages that held the promise of business and had supplied funds for construction. The routing of the main line above Middletown, in fact, was influenced as much, if not more, by the financial attraction of those communities that agreed to bond themselves as it was by geographic necessity or business opportunity. Every deviation made from the projected route, either because of landscape or in avoidance of those communities that refused to provide financial support, was to increase operational and maintenance costs, decrease competitive value and reduce on-line sources of revenue—problems that would far outlive these visionaries.

In the end, they created a 272-mile main line between endpoints (Oswego-Cornwall) that had an air distance of 190 miles. The result was a railroad that would fill regional transportation needs while creating limited regional development, but it had a built-in time limit on its useful life. On June 10, 1873, the new route was placed in service with the operation of a through train that originated in Oswego.

In the broadest sense, then, the NY&OM sprang from forces and currents running though

Like so many locations along the route, the Maywood (N.Y.) station did a great business in dairy products. Borden's eventually operated the large creamery next to the depot, and independent farmers shipped cans directly from the station.—O&W SOCIETY COLLECTION.

Wilber's Siding, ten miles north of Norwich, had an operator's office installed at its north end about 1909. Locomotive 41 is pulling the first section of train 29, the Ontario Central Dispatch, and it is passing through without slowing down for orders. Since the operator is not in sight to inspect the train as it passes, it may be that he is the photographer. Note the extra-high switchstand.
—CLYDE CONROW COLLECTION.

a vibrant expanding nation "flexing its muscles" in the decades following the Civil War. Specifically and regionally, it came into existence as a result of extensive communications and meetings between parties living in those counties that more or less formed a line of route between the eastern end of Lake Ontario and New York City. Although it never became the "Grand Through Route" that its promoters envisioned, the Midland eventually justified its construction after a financial reorganization brought less-visionary (and probably less opportunistic) management.

The line's completion was met with two unfortunate coincidences. First and most immediate was the severe financial and business panic of 1873—America's worst up to that time. Second and more long-term was the start of a decline in the state's rural population, which continued through the latter part of the century. Farm families were moving west to lands made accessible, ironically, by recent railroad construction in that part of the nation.

The new railroad could not meet its fixed charges which included assumption of the NJM's construction debt as well as its rental fee. Within a month of the route's opening, the OM was placed in receivership. The court appointed two men, Abram S. Hewitt and James G. Stevens, to oversee the property. Hewitt was a New Jersey industrialist heavily involved in iron manufacturing and familiar with railroading. During their tenure, the two trustees managed the property in a more businesslike manner, utilized the assets more efficiently and nurtured potential sources of revenue. One of their major decisions was to abandon the effort to reach Lake Erie via the anemic, 85-mile Auburn Branch—which was an afterthought headed for Buffalo.

Six years of prudent management improved

At the top of the grade between Sidney and Norwich was the Summit operator's office, which contained living quarters. Midland surveyors had to plot several half circles to keep grades approaching the 1,600-foot summit within reason.—O&W SOCIETY COLLECTION

the property to the point that it attracted the attention of a group of investors who purchased the company for $4.6 million in 1879 and renamed it the New York, Ontario & Western. In 1880, the new company was able to show a modest but hopeful net profit of $17,500.

Shortly after the O&W was incorporated, its owners became involved in the promotion and construction of the New York, West Shore & Buffalo, a route that eventually would parallel Cornelius Vanderbilt's New York Central & Hudson River all the way to Buffalo via Albany, N.Y. Naturally, NYC&HR viewed the West Shore Line as a nuisance or blackmail scheme.

Complicated financial arrangements existed

(ABOVE) Hoppers by the score occupy the yard on the north side of the Cornwall coal dock. Coal was transshipped to rail connections on the other side of the Hudson as well as to destinations up and down the river. (BELOW) Built in 1908, Western was one of two sea-going tugs in the railroad's marine fleet; the other was the Ontario. Much in the manner of way-freight trains, the tugs would haul strings of coal-laden barges up the New England coast with frequent stops to set one off at a coal dealer's dock.—BOTH PHOTOS, O&W SOCIETY COLLECTION.

City, in 1884. These projects provided the O&W with a more-reliable and more-direct route to the metropolitan area than had been available with the NJM connection.

The O&W-West Shore combination was dissolved when the latter entered bankruptcy in 1884 and was subsequently leased by NYC. The Middletown Branch became part of the O&W, and NYC permitted O&W to continue using the West Shore between Cornwall and Weehawken.

The O&W underwent an administrative reorganization after its involvement with the West Shore came to an end. Thomas P. Fowler, a talented lawyer formerly with NYC's legal department, became the new president. He is reputed to have said that he wondered why the O&W had been built and why, after entering bankruptcy, it hadn't been allowed to stay there. Regardless of his comment, he must have seen some potential in the line, and with the American economy in a period of expansion, he set out to make a respectable property of the NYO&W.

During Fowler's term, the railroad significantly aided in, or undertook the development of, several industries. It firmly established itself as a tourist carrier to the resort hotels and camps in the mountains of Orange, Sullivan and Delaware counties (often referred to as the "lower Catskills"). The road expanded its operations in the haulage of milk and dairy products and, most importantly, it became a carrier of anthracite coal by tapping the northern Wyoming Valley coal field in northeastern Pennsyvlania through the railroad's most-ambitious expansion program: the construction in 1889-90 of the 55-mile Scranton Division.

Most of this coal was to move to northern, northeastern and seaboard markets, much of it by water. Piers were erected at Oswego, Cornwall and Weehawken to transload the coal to ships and barges. A marine department had to be organized and equipped to transport the new business to coastal and Great Lakes customers.

The building of the Scranton line also necessitated the boring of a tunnel north of Walton,

between the O&W and the West Shore which were detrimental to the corporate health of the former. However, this was mitigated by West Shore's construction of a branch from its main line at Cornwall, N.Y., to Middletown in 1883 and by opening terminal facilities in Weehawken, on the Hudson River across from New York

(RIGHT) Firthcliffe was about three miles north of Cornwall and was the first northbound station stop after leaving West Shore tracks. Like many of the depots built by the West Shore between Middletown and Cornwall, it looked more like a Victorian home than a station. The only remaining example of this type of O&W-related architecture is the Mechanicstown station which is now a restaurant on the outskirts of Middletown.
—O&W SOCIETY COLLECTION

N.Y., to eliminate a mainline switchback, and it also required the purchase of additional cars and locomotives to haul the coal as well as additional boxcar freight coming from new connections at and near Scranton.

Other notable and important changes took place during the two decades bracketing 1900. The New Berlin Branch was extended seven miles to reach Edmeston, N.Y., and the Port Jervis, Monticello & New York Railroad was purchased to stifle that railroad's plans to build a competing line to Kingston, N.Y. The Central New England, later a part of the New Haven, built the Poughkeepsie Bridge over the Hudson River and extended its route to Campbell Hall, N.Y., to connect with Erie, NYC, Lehigh & Hudson River, Lehigh & New England and O&W. In 1902, the Kingston Branch was opened as an extension of the Ellenville line and the 35-mile long route, terminating at Kingston, provided a great deal of local business as well as another interchange with NYC.

In 1904, the New Haven, frustrated in its attempt to control the L&HR and thus further expand its influence west of the Hudson, bought a controlling interest in the O&W by purchasing 50.8 percent of the common stock. This provided the New Haven with some leverage for rate dealings with connections in the New York metropolitan area as well as a link to the anthracite region. The steadily increasing coal traffic required double-tracking of the main line all the way from Mayfield Yard (Scranton) to Cornwall.

Through a combination of new track construction and trackage rights over the Delaware, Lackawanna & Western about 1905, a coal branch was extended to a connection with the Lehigh Valley at Sibley Junction, Pa., just west of Scranton. This junction was important for coal business and later as part of a bridge route for through traffic.

In 1912 Thomas Fowler resigned and the acquisitive Charles S. Mellon, president of the New Haven, assumed the same position on the O&W but served for only one year. He was succeeded by John B. Kerr who had the distinction of presiding over the railroad during a busy period of extensive physical improvement and business expansion in the years immediately prior to World War I. During the latter part of World War I, the O&W, along with all major American railroads, was placed under the control of the United States Railroad Administration (USRA). A year or so after the war ended, the railroads were returned to their owners and Kerr resumed direct management.

Although the coal business wavered in the 1920's, it remained strong into the early years of the Great Depression and it permitted the O&W to continue paying dividends. Nonetheless, petroleum fuels, natural gas and electricity were making ever greater inroads into coal markets. Coal was losing ground, but it definitely was not out. O&W handled only about four percent of the anthracite shipped out of Pennsylvania, but in the early 1930's, this one commodity still accounted for over 50 percent of the railroad's income. But this was an unhealthy situation, one of too great a reliance on one industry.

The decline of coal was not O&W's only dilemma. Economic activity as a whole in the U.S. was changing dramatically. Manufacturing activities were moving to the South, Southwest and West, and the resultant population shifts were changing the consumer markets and the rural economy upon which the early O&W and

The largest of the O&W's four self-propelled passenger rail cars was the 804 which is shown at Summitville. It was the only one with a post office section. At the time, the car was probably assigned to the Summitville-Kingston run, with Port Jervis or Monticello service a less-likely possibility. The car eventually went to the New Haven along with the 802 and 803.—AL SEEBACH COLLECTION

(RIGHT) The Scranton Division way freight crosses Route 17, the Erie main line and the Delaware River at Hancock, N.Y. Two empty milk cars will be spotted at creameries on the upper end of the division as the train works its way down to May-field Yard.—RUSTY RECORDON COLLECTION.

(LEFT) For a brief period near the turn of the century, O&W carried the largest volume of milk into New York City of any railroad. It had a fleet of approximately 150 wooden milk cars in the service. Over 100 of them were similar to the 1008 shown at Middletown in 1938.— GEORGE E. VOTAVA.

its predecessors had relied. What the OM's developers had promised the railroad would do had occurred; but it was Western railroads opening Western lands to agricultural development that better filled the promise. The decline in the importance of the small towns and cities, the expansion of the suburban industrial parks, and the population shifts to metropolitan areas or to other parts of the country were severely felt by "rural roads" such as the O&W.

Beginning in the 1920's (but with a slackening during World War II), much of the milk and passenger traffic shifted to improved highways. With the qualified exceptions of Liberty, Monticello, Walton and Delhi, N.Y., the O&W had no cities or large towns that depended upon it alone for rail service. These towns could hardly be considered industrial centers; in fact it was their lack of industrial activity that had once made them attractive rail vacation destinations.

Unfortunately, too, the O&W did not have a large enough "mixed portfolio" of industries or an adequate, diversified, on-line agriculture base to sustain it through uncertain economic times. There were no wheat, fruit or livestock "rushes" in volumes that, say Great Northern, Union Pacific or Santa Fe accepted year after year. O&W did not serve any Pittsburgh, Buffalo or Kansas City laced with steel mills, flour-mills, refineries or packing houses which shipped thousands of carloads yearly, thus tempering the vagaries of seasons, weather, labor disputes, over- or under-production and the market fluctuations faced by coal.

On Feb. 25, 1937, the O&W advised the holders of its Refunding Mortgage Bonds, due in 1992, that it could not pay the interest due on March 1. Two of the three railroad-owned collieries had earlier defaulted on their loans from the railroad. This, coupled with an overall decrease in anthracite tonnage, reduced freight rates, increased taxes and other increased expenses caused the railroad to default on its financial obligations. As a result, O&W entered a voluntary bankruptcy from which it would not emerge. The O&W was certainly not alone: By mid-1938 almost 40 Class I railroads were in receivership.

The United States District Court for the Southern District of New York assigned Judge Murray Hulbert to O&W's petition and, approving its application, placed the railroad under trusteeship. With approval of both the court and the Interstate Commerce Commission, Frederic E. Lyford was named trustee on July 15, 1937.

By all accounts, Lyford was a talented and capable individual who brought a solid railroad background to the O&W. His program for the rejuvenation of the O&W combined innovation, economy, modernization and traffic solicitation. He used all four in his efforts to turn the O&W into a competitor for bridge traffic to the New York metropolitan area, New England and eastern Canada. Bridge traffic, so named because it would pass over the O&W between its point of origin and its final destination, was a lucrative but time-sensitive business.

Much of this traffic did not have to be switched and was received from and delivered to connecting roads in solid trainloads in short time. A high percentage consisted of foodstuffs, manufactured items and finished products that moved at higher rates than mineral traffic. Bridge traffic required fewer locomotives, yards, manpower and paperwork. It also helped to have a long, flat railroad over which the traffic could be expeditiously forwarded.

The region already had a number of railroads which were in this very business and much better situated to attract and keep bridge traffic. Nonetheless, O&W at this point had few options. There did not seem to be, nor were there likely to be, any new major on-line sources of revenue, and the O&W had only a limited ability to adapt to the changing manufacturing and distribution patterns of the 20th Century. Thus, O&W began focusing on transforming suitable segments of its system into thruways for overhead tonnage, with the Scranton-Maybrook segment as a primary candidate. A secondary bridge route was between Scranton and the NYC at Utica.

It would not be an easy task. O&W's up-and-down vertical profile and constantly curving route limited the speed required to compete for bridge traffic. Further, such movements interchanged with both LV and DL&W were complicated by having to, in part, pass over branch trackage as well as the tracks of competing railroads, from whom permission had to be obtained prior to every movement. It was especially awkward and time-consuming to make connections at LV's Coxton Yard at Pittston, Pa., near Wilkes-Barre. O&W trains had to use a section of busy DL&W track, climb along the side of a mountain and run around at the end of a switchback to get onto LV's Austin Branch which finally led to Coxton Yard.

DL&W and LV were O&W's primary connections for traffic heading to or from the west, but they were also two of its strongest competitors. Both roads interchanged with the Lehigh & Hudson River, which also connected with the New Haven at Maybrook Yard. Although slower through routes, DL&W and LV had marine operations in New York Harbor, enabling them to float their New England traffic across to New Haven's Bay Ridge and Oak Point yards in New York City. Additionally, DL&W and LV connected with Jersey Central, Erie and D&H in the Scranton/Wilkes-Barre corridor, and those roads also had New England connections.

The final shortcoming was that O&W's line haul for New England traffic was rather short. The Scranton-Maybrook distance was 146 miles and thus the rate division for an interline haul was small, especially when applied to a car of California fruit, Oregon lumber or Iowa beef. (A rate division was the percent of the shipping cost paid to each railroad over which a car passed between origin and destination).

What tonnage the O&W did have or could further attract only utilized approximately half of the road's route mileage (569 miles in 1929). Most of the other half was not bringing in enough business to support itself and probably should have been abandoned. On the plus side, much of the bridge-route sections were double-tracked and had automatic signals.

In spite of its limitations, the road made a spirited effort to get and hold the through business. Off-line freight solicitation agencies were

A southbound freight rattles and rolls through Middletown behind a 2-8-0 spraying coal smoke and cinders over the neighborhood while the Wickham Avenue crossing watchman takes in the show. In the distance, stored passenger equipment occupies the yard tracks in front of the station—RAY W. BROWN COLLECTION

established, promotional advertising material was distributed and train schedules were carefully coordinated with connecting roads. An attractive eight-page booklet was published and gave the impression that the O&W's rugged profile had been conquered by spectacular engineering in the manner of the Virginian Railway or the Pittsburgh & West Virginia:

"The construction of the NYO&W, with its tunnels driven through solid rock and its long high bridges, was a difficult and expensive engineering accomplishment. However, it made possible the fast, consistent schedules of today's trains, expediting everything from raw materials needed in the production of implements of war, to meats and fresh vegetables for many a New England household."

Track speed was increased where possible by upgrading roadbed and bridges, and supervisory personnel carefully monitored the movements of trains handling the time-sensitive bridge traffic. Dispatchers' sheets were reviewed daily to maintain the best possible train performance, and corrective actions, insofar as they were within O&W's abilities, were taken when necessary.

Other improvements included the rebuilding

of Weehawken piers to allow O&W to handle other business in addition to the small, remaining volume of coal. During World War II, the rebuilt piers would handle great tonnages of bauxite arriving from Caribbean ports. Most of it was shipped in hopper cars to Sidney, N.Y., for interchange to the D&H, which forwarded it to a Canadian National connection. Mountains of this aluminum ore were stockpiled at the under-utilized Middletown and Cadosia coal-storage plants.

In the process of revamping the railroad, Lyford did not forget the northern end of the O&W. The railroad invested $80,000 in modernization and improvements to the Oswego dock and waterfront property in an effort to attract bulk tonnages. To a degree the plan worked, bringing in lake steamers from the upper Great Lakes. The Oswego gateway would also serve the defense effort during World War II by offering a combined rail/water inland routed that avoided enemy submarines in the Atlantic.

O&W's declining passenger service, unfortunately, could not effectively play into Lyford's plans of rejuvenation. Nonetheless, there had been one passenger-related event that coincided Lyford's arrival as trustee and thus in part served

Frederic E. Lyford

IT WAS HARD TO AVOID RAILROADS in our hometown of Waverly, N.Y. The busy east-west main lines of both the Erie and the DL&W crossed the Lehigh Valley, and just a mile south of that crossing were LV's main shops and yards at Sayre, Pa.

Upon finishing studies at Waverly High School, my father, Frederic E. Lyford, attended Cornell University where he received a degree in mechanical engineering. His first job was apprentice shipfitter with Bethlehem Steel at Sparrows Point, Md. From 1917 to 1919 he was a first lieutenant in the army.

After the war he became an assistant sales manager with Allied Machinery Co. in New York City. He married my mother Eleanor in 1920 and returned to Waverly where he handled sales promotion for the Tioga Feed Mills. His railroad career began shortly afterward with the position of apprentice instructor for the LV at Sayre. He soon progressed to assistant general machine foreman, special engineer to the superintendent of motive power and, finally, special engineer to the executive vice president.

With the Depression, Frederic had to leave the LV but soon was hired by the Reconstruction Finance Corporation as an examiner in the railroad division. He stayed in this position from 1933 until 1936. The job kept him away from home for weeks at a time as he traveled over the U.S. helping railroads weather the dark days of financial stress. In mid-sum-

mer of 1936, he left the RFC for the position of assistant to the vice-president of the Baldwin Locomotive Works in Philadelphia. Our family barely had time to settle into a house in Drexel Park before he took the position of trustee with the NYO&W in 1937, and we moved to Scarsdale, N.Y.

During his O&W tenure, Frederic had employed the marine construction firm of Merritt, Chapman & Scott to rebuild railroad facilities on both Lake Ontario and the Hudson River. It may have been this contact with the company that led to his working for them later. Frederic may also have been among those who saw that railroading was in for tremendous changes after the war and that the weaker lines ultimately would not survive. Whatever his reasons, in 1944 my father resigned from the O&W trusteeship and became assistant to Thomas Scott of Merritt, Chapman & Scott.

As a result of Louie Wolfson's controversial takeover of Merritt, Chapman & Scott in the late 1940's, my father left the company and established the engineering consultancy of Lyford & Eberle. This firm was dissolved in 1951. He then became a consultant with the New York State Commission on Engineering Laws until he retired. He had remarried after the death of my mother in 1957, and in 1975 moved from Scarsdale to Texas where he lived for six years until his death at the age of 86.—NANCY LYFORD

(ABOVE) Diesels only delayed the inevitable for the O&W. In March 1957—the final month for O&W—this anemic FT-powered freight was about to head north from Cadosia.—DAVID CONNOR. (RIGHT) Caboose 8352 trails a southbound freight diving into Hawk Mountain Tunnel. L&HR and O&W were the only two regional lines to stay with wooden-superstructure cabooses throughout their histories. O&W's cabooses deviated from standard "anthracite road" design. The front and rear of the cupola were metal-sheathed. One side had a smaller third window for an enclosed toilet facility, but there was no belt-driven generator, oil nor gas heat, refrigeration or electric marker lamps.—T. J. DONAHUE. (BELOW) O&W F-units idle beside a handsome set of Lehigh New England Alco FA's on a freight at Maybrook Yard. Trustee Frederick Lyford was responsible for transforming the O&W into a bridge carrier, and Maybrook was a key component of that plan, offering O&W a direct connection to New England via the New Haven.—GUY TWADDELL.

An aerial post-abandonment view of the Middletown shop and yard complex shows three semi-circular fields to the left of center that mark the old coal storage yard. Lines of cabooses and wooden work equipment sit just north of the Wisner Avenue crossing and several rows of diesel locomotives can be seen on the far side of the erecting shops. Much of the yard trackage had been lifted in the previous decade and the roundhouse and various smaller buildings, for the most part, had already outlived their usefulness.—O&W SOCIETY COLLECTION

as a sort of herald of O&W's impending new era: the June 24, 1938, debut of the *Mountaineer Limited*, a summer-season flyer clad in maroon, orange and black that ran between Weehawken and Roscoe for the benefit of summer tourists. Input from hotel and boarding-house owner associations led to improved scheduling and train operation for the vacation trade, and, despite the recent bankruptcy, O&W budgeted $10,000 for the *Mountaineer* project (see pages 22-23).

The decline in O&W's passenger revenues slowed during World War II, but little could be done to slow the dollar loss on long-distance service. In 1948, passenger runs were cut back to Roscoe, the remaining service primarily accommodating the vacation trade out of the New York City metropolitan area. Year-round service ended in 1950, and passenger trains were totally eliminated at the end of the 1953 summer season.

In 1940, the New York, Susquehanna & Western, like O&W, was also undergoing reorganization, and the two roads recognized that mutual aid was possible in cooperation. Susquehanna, breaking away from Erie control, needed another party to perform a variety of administrative, operational and maintenance functions until it could re-establish such departments for itself. O&W accepted these responsibilities, charging a more modest fee to perform them than Erie. Using the 14-mile Middletown & Unionville (both roads repeating the 1870's practice of their predecessors), a marginally successful through route was also re-established between the two lines.

Under Lyford, the road continued to have limited luck with encouraging new businesses to locate on line. Hope seemed to spring eternal as the railroad's sales and traffic people knocked on

any door that offered another carload of freight, but once the traffic was garnered, there was the problem of determining rate divisions. O&W had to carefully find the balance between asking for a division that the connection lines thought too high and one that was too little to justify the effort expended in moving the car. This was an important consideration because connecting lines had routing discretion for those cars whose routing the shipper left open. There was a definite "quid pro quo" aspect to getting business, and the O&W, as traffic density maps make clear, had few westbound loads to trade for north- and eastbound cars.

Statistics compiled for 1943 and compared with 1938 showed that the company had increased its overall freight revenue by 33 percent based upon the following: Freight tonnage passing over the line as bridge traffic was up 252 percent; originating and terminating (intraline) tonnage was down 45 percent; originating interline tonnage was up 27 percent; and terminating interline tonnage was up five percent. In 1936, anthracite coal represented 67.4 percent of O&W's freight revenue and amounted to more than $5.1 million. Merchandise freight that year brought in nearly $4.5 million. By 1944, anthracite revenue was down to just less than $2 million, and merchandise traffic—accounting for 76 percent of total freight carried—brought in just over $6.1 million. Clearly, the railroad had made impressive progress under Lyford's efforts, and it could not be attributed to war traffic alone.

NYO&W reported the following as the commodities that were bringing in the greatest revenues, in order of importance, in 1944:

1. anthracite coal
2. iron, steel and scrap

3. petroleum products
4. paper, including newsprint
5. grain and grain products
6. ores and concentrates
7. bituminous coal
8. sand, gravel and cement
9. lumber and roofing material
10. packing house products
11. canned food
12. autos, trucks and parts

Also listed were the ten most important industries served.

1. Van Storch Colliery, Park Place, Pa.
2. Armstrong Cork, Arrowhead, N.Y.
3. Northwest Coal Company, Forest City, Pa.
4. William A. Colliery, Sibley Junction, Pa.
5. St. Regis Paper Co., Oswego, N.Y.
6. Peter-Cailler-Kohler Co., Fulton, N.Y.
7. Cooperative G.L.F. Exchange (with 16 stores throughout the O&W system)
8. Supreme Anthracite Colliery, Peckville, Pa.
9. Volney Felt Mills, Fulton, N.Y.
10. Crawford Brothers, Walton, N.Y.

World War II provided O&W with a boost in revenues, and two years of profitable operations gave rise to what we may now see as false hopes. Commendable as Lyford's work was, however, the gains achieved during his trusteeship were modest when viewed in the context of the whole rail industry. The termination of wartime exigencies might also have meant the termination of the O&W, with its role in national defense being its finale.

But it wasn't. And Lyford and dieselization were the significant reasons why.

As a progressive railroader, Trustee Lyford followed the advances in diesel-electric locomotive research, development and application. Believing that this form of motive power was no longer experimental and that it could have significant impact upon the affairs of the O&W, he convinced the bankruptcy court to approve the purchase of a small fleet of diesel-powered General Electric light switchers.

Delivered in 1941-42, the five diesels exceeded expectations dramatically. Satisfied with the performance and savings of the switchers, Lyford in 1943, or possibly earlier, initiated a study to see whether mainline freight diesel locomotives could bring new and greater savings in operation as well as additional through freight business. Studies concluded that, if the road were to fully dieselize, it would realize an annual savings $1.5 million—a savings of approximately 19 percent over the cost of steam operations.

Lyford formally announced a dieselization proposal, which bore the approval of both mortgage and bondholders, on June 28, 1944. An order was signed with the Electro-Motive Division of General Motors for road diesels that would begin replacing larger steam power. Having gotten a strong reorganization under way, including the groundwork for the diesels that were to make the O&W more efficient and competitive, Lyford stepped down in December 1944, leaving the completion of his plans to his successors.

Despite his best efforts, a cooperative and sympathetic bankruptcy court and the increased volume of freight traffic that those efforts and the war generated, Lyford was probably dubious that the O&W could ever be reorganized successfully. The line was becoming more of a transportation anachronism whose survival was increasingly questionable. Undoubtedly, though, diesels were key to extending the life of the NYO&W. The dieselization process that Lyford launched in 1941 and accelerated in 1944 was hardly a cut-and-dried procedure, as readers will shortly see.

THE COURT APPOINTED Lyford's former executive assistant and vice-president of operations, Raymond L. Gebhardt, to the trusteeship. Ferdinand J. Sieghardt, a co-trustee, was appointed to serve with him. Like Lyford, Gebhardt was a former Lehigh Valley employee, and he came to the O&W in July 1941 at the behest of his former colleague. Gebhardt played a large role in the dieselization studies and concurred with trustee's plans for motive-power replacement. Sieghardt was a businessman whose appointment was pressed by the holders of various O&W securities in hopes he would aid in business and industrial development.

With the end of the war came the anticipated decrease in both freight and passenger revenue. The railroad searched through its departments and procedures to find ways to cut costs. Money- and time-saving Centralized Traffic Control (CTC) was one answer. Short segments of this train-control system had been installed before the

Number 253, a Camelback 4-6-0, takes a northbound passenger train past a section house and the foundation of the Rock Tavern creamery. A steel combine and five coaches are shrouded in coal smoke which is undoubtedly annoying the passengers. —GERRY BERNET COLLECTION.

war and had proven successful in reducing the need for double-track, operators and telegraphers. Thus, after the war, CTC was installed for much of the distance between Middletown and Cadosia, the busiest segment of the railroad.

Consolidation and elimination of departments and personnel also helped to trim losses. This resulted in deferred maintenance—which, in many areas, was never resumed. Coal, milk and passenger revenues, already in decline before the war, continued to drop. By the late 1940's, the extensive Middletown and Cadosia coal-storage plants were closed, as were the coal docks at Oswego and Cornwall.

Several plans were proposed for abandoning various sections of the railroad, but with the exception of the sale of the New Berlin Branch to the Unadilla Valley Railway in 1941, virtually no route mileage was sold or removed from service.

Despite continuing losses, there was still great hope that further modernization with improved levels of service could save the railroad.

Late in 1947, orders were placed with EMD for 28 additional units to complete the dieselization. These arrived in 1948, permitting the total retirement of steam facilities and many employees, and the last pungent haze of coal smoke disappeared from the property. However, within a year the trustees, in reaction to an employees' strike, petitioned for complete abandonment. The 1949 strike, called by the operating unions, shut the O&W down. The National Mediation Board arranged a six-month fact-finding period and appointed James P. Kiernan, a neutral observer, to make a survey of the railroad. His report made public many of the shortcomings that were well known within the company and among rail shippers.

The Mountaineer Limited ⓦ

FREDERIC LYFORD, *appointed trustee of the O&W in 1937, knew the railroad business and knew marketing. The hotels and resorts of the lower Catskills (often referred to as the "Borscht Belt") had developed as a result of the railroad's entry into the region and provided a steady, if largely seasonal, passenger business. Lyford felt that a glamorized "name" train would be needed to compete with the ever-increasing private auto traffic as well as buses and the limousines (known locally as "hackers") that were operating between New York City and the mountains.*

Otto Kuhler, a German-born industrial designer who came to the U. S. in the 1920's, had made a reputation for his design work on diesel switchers at the American Locomotive Company. This was quickly followed by the headline-making Hiawathas of the Milwaukee Road and B&O's Royal Blue. Kuhler learned of Lyford's interest in a budget streamlining of an O&W train and accepted a small commission from the railroad. Surveying the O&W route, Kuhler had to take into account the numerous tunnels when choosing a livery. Pleased with the effect he had achieved with orange, maroon, light gray and black on the Hiawathas, he applied them all to the Mountaineer except the light gray since it would have quickly shown soot picked up from passage through the tunnels.

The streamstyling of the engine consisted of simple sheet steel side panels along the running board and a front bib between the pilot braces. On this bib an etched stainless-steel O&W herald was set in a black background flanked by orange Art Deco wings. A chromed bell was mounted on the smoke box front and was complemented by chromed handrails and twin exhaust stack bands.

The only other sheet-metal additions were Art Deco wings on the two observation car tailgates on each side of rectangular steel plaques on which the O&W herald was painted. The budget was so severe that but one tail sign declaring THE MOUNTAINEER LIMITED was made. It was carried to the rear of the train before each run and was bolted over the rectangular plaque on the tailgate of the observation car that was being used.

Kuhler stated that he did not like to be restrained in his designs, yet the $8,500 budget resulted in one of his most aesthetically pleasing works. Engine 405 was selected from the ten Y-class 4-8-2's to receive the renovations and afterward was referred to by some fans as the "Red Devil." Deep maroon was used on the locomotive bib, side panels, pilot beam, cylinders, pilot and drive wheels, cab and tender sides up to, and in line with, the cab eaves. Orange accents were found on the maroon pilot beam, wings on the bib, cab number and tender initials and as one-inch stripes on the side panels, pilot wheels, driver hubs and tires. Three additional one-inch stripes—reminiscent of a Brooks Brothers suit—were applied to the lower tender sides. These were carried

The Mountaineer's combine and one coach are being inspected in this scene at Middletown shops, possibly prior to the train's inauguration.—O&W SOCIETY COLLECTION

Clearly, an attitude of resignation—perhaps analogous to a sports team that has successive poor seasons—was apparent. The faith in the line's strategic value was fading as alternatives to its uncertain services were found or created. This reduced the company's political importance to government and its stature within the railroad industry. This ever-enlarging downward spiral was reflected in the company's financial statistics.

The abandonment request was denied, but the fact-finding report, critical of the trustees, did not motivate much positive change. Gebhardt died early in 1953, and Sieghardt resigned at the end of the year. On March 9, 1954, Lewis D. Freeman, the last chief of the Railroad Division of the Reconstruction Finance Corporation, became the fourth and final trustee to attempt a reorganization of the property.

As was true of the O&W's first trustee, Free-man was also familiar with the railroad's situation through his work in the RFC. He had in fact approved the extension of credit to the company to purchase the GE switchers and later (in a twist of irony) had been a principal in unsuccessful government proceedings to repossess the EMD diesels. This occurred when the road defaulted on its equipment trust obligations only a few years before his arrival in Middletown.

Since 1937, every plan of reorganization had been rejected by either the court or the ICC as being unworkable or impractical. In only two years did income exceed operating expenses: Approximately $200,000 net was achieved in both 1942 and 1943. From then on, wage increases, rising costs of supplies and maintenance and increasing competition took every dollar of income and then some. Attempts to sell the entire O&W under the condition of continued opera-

(LEFT) In the only known color photo of the Mountaineer, *the train is the center of attention while serving in excursion service at Scranton on May 25, 1941.—PAUL LUBLINER COLLECTION. (BELOW) Ulster was one of two observation cars upgraded for Mountaineer service.—CAL'S CLASSICS.*

through the length of the train. Car sides were maroon with a black window band between the maroon vestibule doors. Roofs, underbodies and ends were black.

An orange herald with single trailing wing was painted on each side of the combine. Steel coaches 282-285, combine 127, and coach-observation cars Ulster and Orange made up the Mountaineer's rolling stock. Their interiors were painted in ivory and gray with red accents. Tan slip covers with printed green winged O&W heralds covered each seat. Simple maple armchairs were installed in the observation cars, and the original wooden paneling was retained. Due to a cost of some $10,000 per car, air conditioning was not installed and the heat, dust and cinders still had to be endured.

Through creative use of color, some sheet metal and modest interior redecoration, Kuhler had achieved an eye-catching

economy version of larger railroads' streamliners and brought a new burst of publicity and patronage to the O&W. From the first revenue run on June 24, 1938, until its demise four years later because of the war, the autumn-hued Mountaineer

brought the O&W and its employees, passengers and on-line communities a bit of excitement and pleasure that is still fondly remembered by those fortunate enough to have witnessed its colorful but brief passage—PAUL LUBLINER.

23

(RIGHT) In a soon-to-end ritual (at least on the O&W), a mother and her son savor the arrival and departure of southbound O&W passenger train No. 2 at Cornwall on Sunday, Sept. 6, 1953, four days before the end of passenger service. The tourist season is just about over, and shortly O&W will return the leased coaches on this train to the NYC—forever.
—JOHN F. MINKE III.

(ABOVE) The NYC operator at CN tower in Cornwall holds up the order fork to the fireman of a northbound O&W passenger train; the West Shore main line curves to the right. The grassy appearance of the O&W main reflects reduced maintenance between this point and Campbell Hall. With the end of the coal business, little through or local freight and a soon-to-be-terminated summer passenger traffic, the manpower and maintenance dollars went to busier sections of the railroad.—CHET STEITZ COLLECTION

tion were unsuccessful, and piecemeal-purchase bids were judged unacceptably low to cover bondholders' interests. The perennial sales of parcels of land, unneeded buildings, scrap rail, old cars, shop machinery and locomotives could not go on indefinitely and certainly were no substitute for income-producing freight traffic.

The indebtedness continued to build and by 1955 was reported to be over $100 million, which included over $7.5 million owed to the federal government. All levels of government—federal, state, county and local—seemed to be losing both patience and interest in the O&W, and more than one creditor, mortgagee or bondholder asked the court one or more times to liquidate the property before additional asset deterioration occurred.

On Jan. 7, 1957, the long-standing order barring actions by leinholders and creditors was lifted, permitting the federal government to pursue tax claims which had been accruing since 1945. This action, with the subsequent appointment of receivers, ended the reorganization proceedings. A few weeks later, the court, under Judge Sylvester Ryan, directed trustee Freeman to relinquish the business to receivers James B. Kilsheimer and Jacob B. Grumet on Feb. 9.

An effort was made to meet a court-imposed

60-day final moratorium for getting the line on a profitable footing, but the receivers, under court pressure, were more concerned with liquidation than with the operation of a railroad. A grassroots campaign managed to raise more than $200,000 for continued operations, a powerful footnote on the line's impact on the community. However, it was only a drop in the proverbial bucket and could not solve the larger problem. On March 29, 1957, the locomotives were shut down, marker lights and switch lamps extinguished, doors locked, and the 77-year life of the New York, Ontario & Western came to an end.

Could the line have survived if it had been carefully pruned of the money-losing route-mileage and attention then directed to the bridge-route sections? Were there any untapped traffic sources? It's doubtful that there was ever a game lost or a business gone bankrupt that has not been through the "what if" scenario. Most of the railroad's friends and critics were too close to the event to view it in a detached manner. Other people had money invested in O&W securities or had depended upon it for taxes, or looked to its presence for secondary economic support. These conditions cloud the rational and unemotional economic factors that determine the success or failure of a business. As the years passed, though, it was clear that those needing O&W's services decreased as the outdated, increasingly inefficient, labor- and maintenance-intensive railroad was left behind by an ever more modern age.

That age and every age required changes in order for a business to remain competitive. While under trusteeship, the O&W met some of the imposed changes with some success, but eventually it reached the limits of its ability to do so. It is amazing that the road managed to cling to life well after it had reached that limit. Its "life

(RIGHT) This freight-traffic density schematic from 1953, after dieselization, shows traffic as it stood pretty much to the end of the O&W's existence. As had been the case since the Lyford era, traffic was heaviest between Mayfield Yard and Maybrook/Campbell Hall. Although traffic had dropped overall systemwide after World War II (see graphs), the drop was especially precipitous between Cornwall and Weehawken. In 1938, for example, O&W had hauled some 1.5 million tons of freight into Weehawken; in 1953, the amount was down to a paltry 50,000 tons. Also note the lopsided traffic flow, with more tons moving east than west.

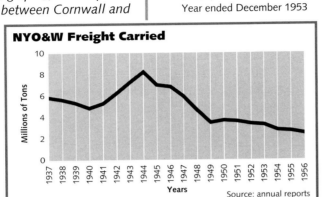

NYO&W Freight Carried

Millions of Tons / Years

Source: annual reports

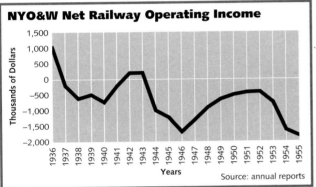

NYO&W Net Railway Operating Income

Thousands of Dollars / Years

Source: annual reports

Graphs: Rusty Recordon and Rick Johnson

support" system was the patience of many creditors, the protection of the United States District Court and—to a degree—the new diesel fleet. But the financial hemorrhaging could not continue indefinitely.

Railroads were literally built through—and upon—rock. Every passing year more permanently imprinted a railroad's roadbed into the earth and into the regional psychology. Railroads were pillars of America's industrial strength, and although they might have illnesses, it was virtually inconceivable to a region (and probably to the nation) that one could die. The O&W's demise in 1957 was the first wholesale abandonment of a major U.S. railroad—and a signal to the industry that the unthinkable was indeed possible.

But the fact that the O&W had tenaciously lingered on the verge of death so long and had stubbornly refused to make the final gasp was, strangely, an indication of its permanence in the scheme of things. Something that loomed so large—physically, financially, psychologically and even emotionally—in the lives of so many people could not easily be let go.

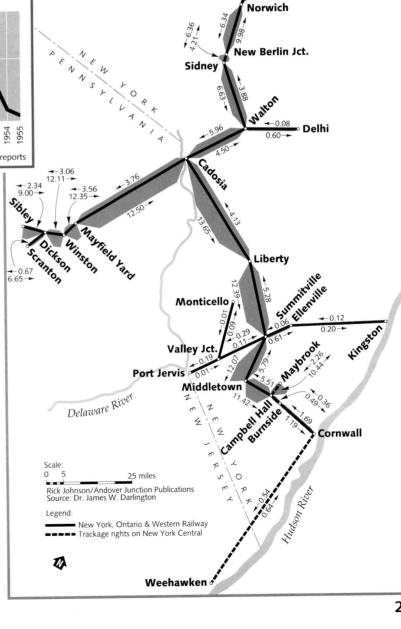

New York, Ontario & Western Railway

Freight traffic density
in 100,000 tons
Year ended December 1953

Scale:
0 5   25 miles
Rick Johnson/Andover Junction Publications
Source: Dr. James W. Darlington

Legend:
—— New York, Ontario & Western Railway
----- Trackage rights on New York Central

2/O&W Motive Power

At the time of its completion in 1873, the New York & Oswego Midland and its affiliated New Jersey Midland rostered nearly 100 locomotives. The fleet was predominantly 4-4-0 and 2-6-0 types built by Rhode Island Locomotive Works and Baldwin Locomotive Works, with a small number coming from other builders. The first locomotives that had been delivered, in 1869, were 14 wood-burning 4-4-0 American types that wore gilt trim and names (selected from on-line towns and counties) as well as numbers. Some of these locomotives arrived via canal boat and underwent final assembly at the point of delivery.

The next group of engines came in 1870 and were split between wood and coal burners. That order saw the arrival of the 2-6-0 Moguls for road work and the 0-4-0 wheel arrangement for switching purposes. By 1872, it appeared that the wood burners were converted to coal, and all subsequent orders were for coal burners. Also in that year, a pair of 2-8-0's (Consolidations) were delivered, allegedly for pusher service.

Following the Midland's bankruptcy in 1873, shortly after the railroad was completed, the roster quickly began to shrink as builders took back locomotives to satisfy unpaid bills. Likewise, the NJM, freed from OM control, retrieved several it had contributed to the joint roster. In spite of these losses, the struggling Midland still had more than enough locomotives to meet its service needs through the period of receivership—enough so that the railroad could shove each worn-out engine onto the repair track and replace it with a relatively new one. Although this deferred maintenance reduced the cost of operations—at the time of OM's sale to NYO&W interests, the Midland roster was down to 79 engines—the new company was saddled with the costs of heavy repairs for many locomotives.

Despite this handicap, the NYO&W managed to get underway with locomotives on hand and did not need to buy any additional motive power until 1886 and 1887. The road then acquired a number of West Shore 2-8-0's and eight new 4-4-0's. New orders and rebuildings of earlier engines produced both new and updated 2-6-0's which handled a large share of both freight and passenger work. The 2-6-0 wheel arrangement was quite popular with the O&W, and its final form for the road arrived from the Cooke Works in 1909 and remained on the property until 1947.

Although the O&W never built any of its own locomotives, it did undertake many rebuilding programs—several resulting in the conversion of 2-6-0's to 4-6-0's in both single-cab and "Camelback" (also known as "Mother Hubbard") versions. The road had a strong affinity for the Camelback design because it permitted the use of a large firebox to burn cheaper, lower-grade fuel. Additional classes of 2-8-0's arrived in the 1890's and around 1910 along with a small group of single-cab 4-6-0's. The last group of 2-8-0's were the versatile W-class engines that performed tasks similar to those of the general-purpose diesels at a later age.

The O&W didn't own many true switcher-type steam locomotives. Outside the few inherited from OM, the road had but one switcher category, the L-class camelback 0-6-0's. Prior to the arrival of the 2-10-2 Santa Fe types in 1915, O&W didn't have a single locomotive that required a trailing truck. The 2-10-2's were drag freight engines best suited to low-speed coal trains, heavy mine switching and helper assignments where their small drivers and 71,000-pound tractive effort made them most useful.

The last two groups of steam power were the 4-8-2's of the Y and Y-2 classes built in the early and late 1920's. Each group consisted of ten locomotives that were used in dual service, although the Y-2's were found more often on freight trains. Half of each group was retired from service and sold to other roads when the first road diesels arrived in 1945.

In the mid-1920's, the railroad dabbled with internal-combustion power with the purchase of

(FACING PAGE) Both of O&W's F-unit groups—the FT's and the F3's—are represented in this memorable scene of a northbound rumbling high above the Mamakating River on Ferndale trestle, near Liberty, N.Y., on June 26, 1954. The F3A/FT&AB provided up to 4200 h.p. to its freight, the caboose of which is back in the village of Ferndale.—DAVID CONNOR.

(LEFT) Adversaries face off in Middletown. In the winter of 1947, the 405 takes on coal as an FT set looks on. Within a year, the steam age on the O&W ended. Even at this date, only half of each class of 4-8-2's is still on the roster, and the components for their replacements were already coming together at the Electro-Motive plant near Chicago. Late in the spring of 1948, the completed diesels will arrive and by August the age of steam will be over.—MARV COHEN.

(RIGHT) The NW2 brigade worked with the F-unit fleet in shouldering the bulk of O&W's diesel-era operations. They were used for switching duties and local and branchline runs. NW2 112 is shown at Middletown on March 29, 1957, the very last day of O&W operations.—JOHN STELLWAGEN.

(RIGHT) The 4-4-0 type was built by the hundreds and was the pioneering motive power during the infancy of American railroading. OM No. 12, a wood-burner built by Rhode Island Locomotive Works in 1869, was named the Oxford. In the early years of railroading, and like earlier canal boats and sailing ships, each locomotive was assigned to one individual who was responsible for his charge. Each thus reflected the care and emblems of individuality that their drivers put into them.—AUTHOR'S COLLECTION.

Many steam locomotives were far more colorful than most of us imagine. The 225, although in a black & white photograph, illustrates the degree to which the four locomotives of this class were embellished. The boiler jacket and domes were probably "Russian Iron," a lighter shade of gray. Yards of striping and trim adorn the drivers, walkways, domes and tender. All brass is highly polished and the sum effect was more than visual for even one so skeptical of modern technology as Henry David Thoreau who said, "When I hear the iron horse make the hills echo with his snort like thunder, shaking the earth with his feet, breathing fire and smoke from his nostrils . . . it seems as if the earth had finally got a race now worthy to inhabit it."—O&W SOCIETY COLLECTION.

(RIGHT AND LOWER RIGHT) Nos. 31 and 35 represent original and modernized versions of O&W'S I-class 2-6-0's, respectively. The class was built in 1903 and 1904, and many were rebuilt as 4-6-0's several years later. A few were still in service in the mid-1940's and were used for switching and local freight work, much like the NW2's, their diesel successors. The 31 is at Cadosia and No. 35 is at the Norwich coal dock.—BOTH PHOTOS, JOHN PICKETT.

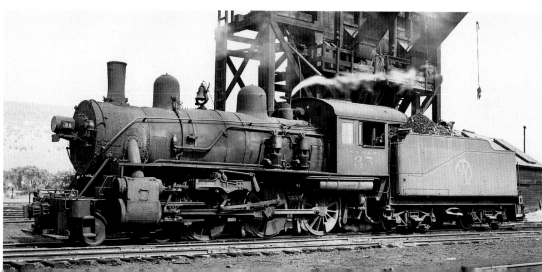

four railcars. The first of these was a Sykes gas-mechanical rail bus and the other three were Brill gas-electric cars. Lower costs per mile made the self-propelled cars attractive replacements for locomotive-hauled locals on several branches and on less-traveled sections of main line. (The road had also considered purchasing a modern American Car & Foundry, self-propelled "Motorailer" in 1940 for winter service on the O&W and summer service on the Susquehanna.) After less than a decade of service, all four cars were retired as both branch and mainline passenger service were reduced. The Brills went to the New Haven and the Sykes was dismantled.

Although the O&W did make numerous contributions to the advancement of railroad technology, its achievements in the development of steam locomotion were hardly spectacular. The trade press reported a number of clever and valuable advancements—one being the improvement of the Baker valve gear—but the line was generally conservative in motive-power experimentation and, for the most part, relied on tried and true appliances. Some of the 2-8-0's and Y-class 4-8-2's were said to be the largest engines of those wheel arrangements when they left the erecting shops of Cooke in Paterson, N.J., or Alco in Schenectady, N.Y. However, such records were very frequently broken in the pre- and post-1900 decades as ever-larger designs were built.

O&W managed to place a distinctive stamp upon its steam motive power after 1900. The above-center headlights, formed sheet-steel stairways leading from pilot deck to running boards, side steps between the cylinder and pilot beam and one or two single-phase air pumps in place

of the more widely accepted cross-compound type gave most classes a unique family appearance. A possible exception was the Y-2 class of 1929. Design costs and construction time were saved when the management decided to copy the L-2c of the New York Central—a road that had ample experience with the 4-8-2 design. In fact, the ten O&W copies were built concurrent with an NYC L-class order. Even at that, however, one was not likely to confuse an O&W Y-2 with a NYC Mohawk.

Piping on O&W power was minimal and the lack of devices such as smokebox-mounted feed-water heaters, number boards and train-control systems permitted the road's power to maintain a cleanliness of design. Although most of these devices were of proven merit and improved the efficiency of locomotives, they frequently did so at the expense of aesthetics.

Neither Pacific nor Mikado types were purchased by the O&W. Pacifics (4-6-2's) were found in passenger service on every major neighboring railroad, but their absence on the O&W was somewhat understandable since the road's passenger service was primarily seasonal. Those few trains which operated year-round were usually light in the winter season and could be easily handled by an E- or W-class locomotive equipped with steam and signal lines for passenger work. As for the Mikados (2-8-2's), apparently the railroad felt it was well able to move both its heavy coal tonnage and handle both yard and road work as well as the occasional extra passenger needs with the 2-8-0's and 2-6-0's on hand. When the time came to consider new motive power in the 1920's, the 4-8-2 had proven itself

(LEFT) Norwich was the home base for a large group of W-class locomotives handling both main- and branchline chores. The 323 has been refitted with a larger tender to increase its operational range. Since the 4-8-2's were not permitted on the Northern Division, the 2-8-0's, singly or in tandem, were the mainline haulers in the late steam age. —JOHN PICKETT

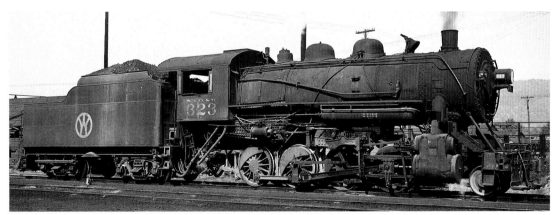

(RIGHT) The seven L-class Camelbacks came to the O&W in 1910-11 for yard and switching services. Their 161,100 pounds, all of it resting on the drive wheels, gave them 34,400 pounds of tractive effort. The small tenders were adequate since the locomotives usually worked near the engine-servicing facilities at which they were based. The 53 was the last steam switcher on the O&W.—JOHN PICKETT.

29

(RIGHT) The diesel that ushered in O&W's dieselization era—GE 44-tonner 101. There are no known color photos of the GE's in their delivered scheme of maroon and silver. This May 27, 1950, photo shows the 101 in its later, traditional O&W livery.—HARRY ZANNIE PHOTO COURTESY OF CHET STEITZ.

(BELOW) On Oct. 20, 1956, the Delhi way freight ambles southward along Route 10 near Hamden, N.Y. Most Delhi Branch traffic consisted of inbound loads of agricultural items. The job usually left Cadosia before daylight and did significant work at Walton in both directions. NW2's were perfect for runs like this.—C. G. PARSONS PHOTO, COURTESY OF BOB'S PHOTOS.

superior to the 2-8-2 design and, for most roads, offered greater versatility.

With the final delivery of Class Y's in 1929, the O&W's steam fleet stabilized. The next search for motive power would come in little more than a decade, but it would be for a significantly different type of locomotive.

O&W TRUSTEE FREDERIC LYFORD was an early believer in dieselization, having watched the evolution of diesel power during the 1930's from that of a curiosity to a major technological advance with potential for tremendous economic importance to railroads everywhere. He became convinced that diesels could have significant positive impact on the future of the O&W and convinced the bankruptcy court likewise. The court approved expenditures for O&W to enter the diesel age. Lyford started with a small step: the purchase of five General Electric 44-tonners.

The versatility and reliability of this switcher had been proven on several railroads and by the operation of a demonstrator unit at several O&W locations. The Reconstruction Finance Corporation (RFC) provided most of the funds for the purchase.

The GE's greatly exceeded expectations despite the fact they were assigned rather limited responsibilities and acted much like in-plant switchers of an industrial operation. Multiple-unit operation (in their early years) and heavy mainline freight haulage was beyond their ability. Satisfied with the performance and savings of the switchers, Lyford initiated a study during the middle years of World War II to see whether mainline freight diesel locomotives could bring new and greater savings in operation as well as additional through freight business. Toward this

(LEFT AND BELOW) The 112 is working the southbound "Pick-Up" on June 26, 1954. It left Liberty moments earlier and is shown approaching, then crossing Ferndale trestle with work to do at a number of towns before tying up at Middletown.—BOTH PHOTOS, DAVID CONNOR.

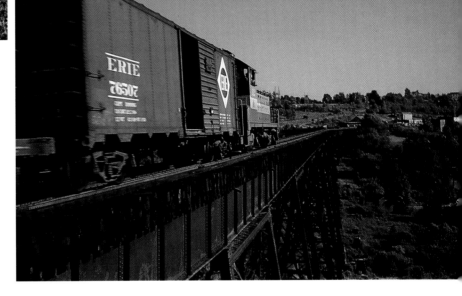

end, he established an in-house team to investigate the possibilities. Colonel Noten D. Ballantine, an individual with an amazingly vast background in railroad consulting, had been employed as an advisor to the trustee since 1938.

With the dieselization studies, Ballantine became transportation assistant to the trustee and headed the efforts. He visited many Western roads and brought back data on performance and costs relative to diesel operations. Other employees made visits to closer railroads to view firsthand the performance and economy of road diesel operations. Like Ballantine, they returned with detailed accounts of over-the-road trips, roundhouse and diesel shop reports and the recorded statements of accountants and officials.

The trustee also called for outside opinions. Coverdale & Colpitts viewed the operational and motive-power requirements in a scenario of fully dieselized operations. Further, it was

(BELOW) "Positions wanted: Prime EMD locomotives looking for work. Experienced, well-groomed, in good mechanical health. Willing to travel. References upon request. Contact receivers, NYO&W Railway, Middletown, N.Y." F-units sit idle at Middletown after the shutdown. Nine went to other roads; seven never worked again.—ROBERT F. COLLINS.

31

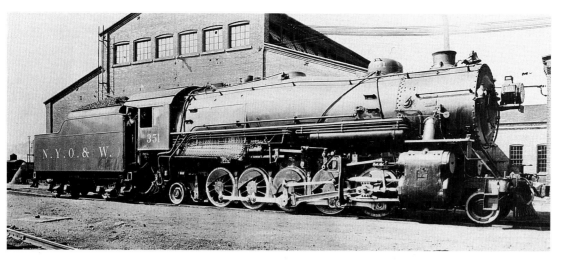

Many disturbing statistics were presented by the facts and conclusions brought in by the company and consultants' reports. To begin, it was determined that, on the average and in size-for-size comparison with O&W power, locomotives on other Class I railroads in the Eastern U.S. could handle about twice the tonnage an O&W

*Ten Class X 2-10-2's, known as the "Bull-mooses," were delivered by Alco in 1915. They were good luggers, but not built for speed and consequently spent their waning years in pusher service.—*HAROLD K. VOLLRATH *PHOTO*

learned that the General Motors' Electro-Motive Division was interested in completely dieselizing a Class I railroad as a means of proving the overall superiority and cost savings of diesel power. EMD was informed that a study of the O&W would be welcome since both the railroad and the locomotive manufacturer shared the same interest in the findings.

EMD assigned a staff engineer, C. T. Zaoral, to lead the study analyzing O&W's unique operating conditions and physical plant and to compute the savings to be realized by replacing all steam power with diesels. This study was made between Feb. 10 and March 18, 1944, and included the assistance of all O&W top- and middle-level operations managers. Although other diesel manufacturers were probably discussed, nothing has been found to indicate that they were asked to submit proposals to the railroad. Of course, much of this had to do with limitations that were enacted by the War Production Board on April 4, 1942, and placed upon diesel manufacturers and other production lines that used scarce and strategic resources.

For most of the war period, only EMD was permitted to produce road freight diesels while other manufacturers were limited to switchers. (An exception was American Locomotive's manufacture of the dual-service, six-axle DL105/DL109/DL110 models.) The WPB's goal was to obtain maximum utilization from existing designs and tooling and to ensure standardization and interchangeability of parts. This war-born edict gave EMD an advantage in road-diesel technology that other manufacturers were never able to overcome.

Zaoral submitted his two-month study in April 1944, and the trustee agreed with the conclusions which stressed the advantages and savings attainable through full dieselization. The estimate came in at $1.5 million—a savings of approximately 19 percent over the cost of steam operations. Lyford's belief that dieselization could partially negate the limitations that geography and the Midland's planners had placed upon the O&W was substantiated by the studies.

locomotive hauled because of the road's physical characteristics. On the road's most heavily used trackage—presumably the Southern Division between Campbell Hall and Cadosia—there were so many curves that every train in effect made the equivalent of a complete 360-degree circle on the average of every 2.7 miles! Further, the combined effect of all ascending grades and curvature resistance equaled 310 feet per mile. To meet these conditions, the O&W required 61 percent more coal to produce 1,000 gross ton-miles than other Class I roads. Most, if not all, Eastern roads had more eastbound loads than westbound. On the O&W it was 120 percent higher, nearly three times greater than on other Class I roads. Helper- and light-locomotive-miles per 100 freight train-miles were also found to be three times greater than the national average.

The numerous bridges (the railroad had 540 of them, of which 209 were over 25 feet long) particularly those of the Northern Division, had limiting weight restrictions which prevented the use of the biggest steam locomotives. Since smaller locomotives had to be used, helper service was necessary over several of the grades.

It was noted, too, that a steam locomotive's horsepower is directly related to its speed with greater tractive force being developed at higher speeds. Due to the physical characteristics of the route, even the O&W's most modern power, the Y and Y-2 classes, could seldom reach a speed where their power could be used to full advantage. Indeed the circumstances when they most needed the pulling power occurred when they were most limited. In comparison, a diesel could develop full horsepower as soon as it stretched draft-gear slack and the train began moving. The trustee stated, "The high-wheel locomotives [Classes Y and Y-2] . . . should never have been purchased for this railroad, as they do not have the characteristics suitable for a railroad with the grade conditions existing on the NYO&W."

At the time of these reports, the railroad operated 87 steam engines that had an average age of 30 years. Older locomotives cost more to repair and operate, and since such costs would increase more rapidly as time went on, it provided further argument for locomotive replacement. In one internal memo, the trustee referred to the steam fleet as "grossly uneconomic to operate." The steam roster was rated at 180,000 horsepower which calculations indicated could be replaced by 74,000 diesel horsepower. (With the arrival of the third and last diesel order in 1948, total diesel horsepower would reach 74,800).

The railroad had another option: the purchase of new, more-efficient steam locomotives to replace the old. It's doubtful that this was very seriously considered. Some type of articulated power had been mentioned in earlier studies, but such power would have required strengthened bridges, larger turntables and modified engine facilities—at a reported cost of over $1 million. There were other strong arguments against new steam power as well.

There are two inherent impacts upon track structure in the operation of steam locomotives. There is a "waddling" or "yawing" effect produced by each power thrust of the pistons. This causes the drivers to slam against the rails in an alternating lateral manner as the engine moves under power. Another impact, called dynamic augment, was vertical. It was caused by the centrifugal action of the driver counterweights and side and main rods. When exerted downward, it increases the pressure of the wheel on the rail, and when acting upward, it tended to lift the wheel from the rail. The pounding, both vertical and horizontal, becomes greater with speed and always created the visible "high centers and low joints" when 39-foot bolted rail sections were the norm. Track surfacing gangs constantly had to tamp ballast under low joints to level the track.

It is easy to imagine the effect of these same pounding forces on the railroad's many trestles. Speed restrictions were necessary on many of them to hold down maintenance costs. Diesels do not deliver power to the wheels in "pulses" as do steam locomotives. As a result, diesel locomotives did not create the pounding forces that were destructive to track, roadbed and bridges. Rather, they provided power to the driving wheels at a continuous torque, resulting in a much lower impact on both track and structures.

As of 1949, half of O&W's mileage was laid with 90-pound rail, and approximately 20 per-

(ABOVE) O&W's final new steam locomotive poses at Alco's Schenectady plant in 1929. The well-proportioned 4-8-2 closely followed the specs of an NYC plan. The ten members of this Y-2 class had a tractive effort of 71,850 pounds which included the assistance of a trailing-truck booster.—O&W Society collection courtesy Alco Historic Photos. (RIGHT) O&W's last steam locomotive purchase was D&H 805, acquired Aug. 9, 1947, to help relieve a motive-power shortage. It had been built in 1903 to specifications very similar to O&W's own P-class 2-8-0's. The 700 number series had been set aside for diesel use, but the 701 was the only locomotive within it.—John P. Ahrens courtesy of Ray W. Brown.

As the graphs below illustrate, dieselization had a marked effect on the O&W's operating costs and related items. Events showed that diesels slowed the dollar loss but could not stop it.

Graphs: Rusty Recordon and Rick Johnson

cent carried 75-pound rail; only twelve miles had 110-pound or heavier steel. Ties were supported primarily by cinders or culm (a waste product of coal mining), and about a quarter of the route mileage rested on sand and gravel. Stretches of more stable and solid crushed rock were quite rare. Heavier rail and more substantial roadbed were better able to support the weight and forces of reciprocating steam power and so required less maintenance attention and dollars. If larger and more-powerful steam power had been purchased back in 1945, an accelerated program of rail replacement and roadbed improvement would also have been

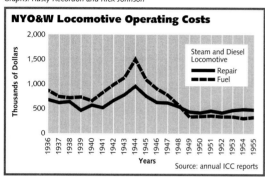

NYO&W Locomotive Operating Costs

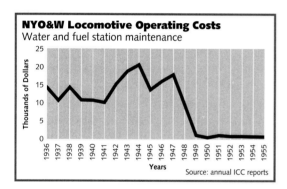

NYO&W Locomotive Operating Costs
Water and fuel station maintenance

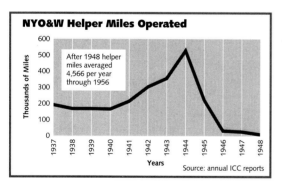

NYO&W Helper Miles Operated

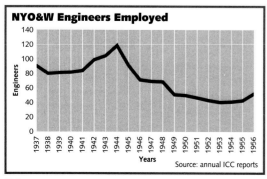

NYO&W Engineers Employed

would also have been required. (EMD pointed out to the company, that because of the diesels' kinder treatment of track, speed restrictions could be exceeded by ten percent if their locomotives replaced steam).

Northfield Tunnel, between Walton and Sidney, had for years presented operational problems, primarily the restriction of X-, Y- and Y-2-class steam locomotives to assignments south of the tunnel account of clearance problems. Although the engines probably could have passed through if they were towed, clearances would likely have been compromised if the engines were operating under their own power—the motion would have caused the cab or the pilot beam to strike the walls of the bore. On the other hand, diesels could pass through unrestricted by lateral motion. There were also limitations created by the two trestles at Sidney Center, Lyon Brook trestle and sundry other structures north of Sidney.

Steam-powered through freights lost

valuable time in adding and uncoupling helper engines, taking on coal and water and cleaning fires. Heavy grades required setting up and turning down retainers and cooling wheels. These latter delays could be eliminated by dynamic brakes, an important optional feature on EMD road diesels. Four-unit diesel locomotives would seldom need helpers on the O&W, nor would they need to take on fuel as often as steamers. Further, when operated in sets with A (cab) units at both ends, time would not be lost in turning locomotives.

Having secured an increase in bridge traffic, the railroad realized that such tonnage required special attention and dependable service if it was to be retained. Diesel power could provide that dependability and at the same time serve as an advertising tool. Competition was strong, and even a percentage of the volume of war traffic would be difficult to hold in peacetime without the substantial improvement in efficiency that diesels could provide. Additionally, O&W's main competitors for bridge traffic—DL&W, LV, Erie and NYC—were all dieselizing, and in spite of its difficulties, the O&W had to present at least a modicum of modernity if it was going to be in the same league. New, streamlined diesels would present visual as well as operational evidence of a railroad that was hard on the comeback trail and counteract the "Old & Weary" image.

The trustee reported that additional freight business was a critical part of a projected income for 1944, which was approximately that for 1943 but in which wages, fuel and other operational costs were adjusted to 1944 levels. After figuring the savings incurred by complete dieselization and including the estimated annual principal payments with interest for the purchase of the diesels, reports projected an annual net income of more than $500,000.

Those holding O&W securities saw the action as necessary for the preservation of the value of the property. A representative of one group of bondholders regarded Lyford ". . . in effect as being able to pull the rabbit out of the hat which will enable this road to take its place not only in theory but in fact as a Class I railroad." The court, as well, clearly believed that dieselization was key to any successful reorganization. Lyford formally announced a dieselization proposal on June 28, 1944.

A $6.7 million order was signed with EMD for 37 diesel locomotives to replace all existing steam power, including several leased locomotives. This agreement was subject to cancellation in whole or in part, thus permitting the railroad to change models and numbers, a privilege which it soon exercised when it was determined that complete dieselization in one transaction was not feasible.

The Zaoral Report and the affidavits in support of Lyford's dieselization plan called for

complete replacement of all steam power. However, in view of the national emergency of the period, as well as the road's credit rating, it quickly became apparent that O&W's dieselization process would have to be spread out over a few years. In one sense, this was good news to the railroad, as the slower conversion would allow for a training period as well as time to convert existing service facilities to road-diesel maintenance bases. Previous experience with the GE 44-ton diesels had already provided a small nucleus of trained mechanics, operators and supervisors, but the changes that would be ushered in by multiple-unit road power would be more encompassing and require more railroaders to change their thinking and work habits.

Zaoral suggested that O&W implement a road-dieselization program with six FT sets (with one "A" and one "B" unit per set), which would be easier to finance and would permit, over a period of time, a more-accurate estimate of the total number of diesels the railroad would actually need. This turned out to be the plan O&W would follow, except that nine instead of six FT sets were acquired; at the same time, the proposed schedule for complete conversion was stretched from one year to three.

The railroad figured that it could raise approximately half the purchase price of the FT's from several sources. Salvage value of the road's steam locomotives was estimated at $200,000 or perhaps higher if some of the more-modern power could be sold on the secondhand market.

However, since the railroad was unable to dieselize all road operations at once, the retirement of steam took place over a period of years during which scores of steam locomotives co-existed with the FT's and 44-tonners.

Similar to its efforts in attempting to finance the GE units a few years earlier, the company could not find a satisfactory commercial source for the larger part of the second dieselization loan. Since it could only raise 25 percent rather than half of the $2,244,074 purchase price of the FT's, the O&W again had to appeal to the Railroad Division of the RFC for help. This effort was successful, and the plan was moving along when Lyford resigned, leaving the O&W for a position with a marine construction and salvage firm. He was replaced by his former executive assistant and vice-president of operations, Raymond L. Gebhardt.

The GE diesels had been in service since 1941, and the FT's arrived in June 1945. Undoubtedly they saved the railroad money, but total dieselization was still the goal. Contact was maintained with EMD, and additional in-house studies were made to see what additional power was needed to replace the remaining steam locomotives. Finally, orders were placed with EMD in 1947 for 28 additional units. The chosen models were the F3, which had superseded the FT, and the NW2 switcher. These arrived in 1948, closing a steam era that had spanned nearly 80 years and commencing an all-diesel era that would last less than a decade.

Rolling past the very offices where many of the considerations and decisions involving dieselization were made, a four-unit set of FT's and F3's roll through Middletown with southbound tonnage bound for Maybrook on July 28, 1949. This impressive diesel quartet seems to impart an undercurrent of optimism for O&W's new era, ushered in by those very decisions.
—GEORGE E. VOTAVA, O&W SOCIETY COLLECTION.

35

3/The GE 44-tonners

O&W dieselized for many general reasons, as the previous chapter outlined. But there were several specific reasons why the road, in 1941, began the process with a modest-size group of small switchers. First, a bankrupt railroad had to be more than reasonably sure of securing a return on a large capital investment, and it was in the diesel locomotive's application to switching that it first achieved success and gained acceptance from the railroad industry. Locomotive reliability and economy in switching service had been conclusively documented, and at least one terminal operation had been completely dieselized by 1940.

Second, dieselization of O&W's largely seasonal passenger service—an alternative option—would have hardly justified the expense despite the fact that a variety of streamlined passenger locomotives (and trains) had proven their merits on several systems in the 1930's. The O&W's own experiences with three gas-electric cars during that same decade appear to have been only marginally successful, although that appears due to the public's abandonment of rail service rather than mechanical shortcomings.

Third, the road freight diesel, in the form of Electro Motive's FT, had only recently (1939) been developed and had yet to establish a reputation for reliability. The same was true of Alco's new road-switcher, the RS1. Normally, such radically new concepts required years of trial and analysis before gaining acceptance from a conservative industry, although a war emergency would accelerate the railroads' acceptance of road freight diesels.

SEVERAL YEARS BEFORE all of the facts about diesel-powered transport fell into place, the O&W had to decide what to do about several classes of steam locomotives that had been suggested for retirement. These classes were listed in a report complied by Superintendent of Motive Power R. G. McAndrew dated April 1937. The locomotives in question were mainly used for yard and

(FACING PAGE) Publicity photos of O&W's new GE's were taken near Fulton, N.Y., and used in GE advertising to promote the sale of 44-tonners. The harsh winter weather of the region tested the mettle of the new locomotives, as fine, wind-blown snow and ice crystals could be a problem to their electrical gear. It's a sure bet enginemen appreciated the more-comfortable cabs and the lack of soot, cinders and smoke. We may wonder, however, just how well the 101 is doing with ten cars and slippery rail. (ABOVE) On Dec. 12, 1941, three locomotives of O&W's five-unit order stand ready for delivery. Bankruptcy-enforced austerities did not extend to locomotive paint schemes. Here was modernity, the hope for better times, and a bold step into the new technology.—BOTH PHOTOS, GENERAL ELECTRIC, O&W SOCIETY COLLECTION. (ABOVE) Mechanical department blueprints noted the basic specifications, including minimum curve ability (50-foot radius) and maximum speed (35 mph).—AUTHOR'S COLLECTION

local switching: Class I (2-6-0), I-1 (4-6-0), P (2-8-0), S (a single 2-8-0 of this class remained), U (2-6-0), U-1 (4-6-0) and V (2-6-0).

Conspicuous by their absence from the list were the L-class 0-6-0 switchers, small Camel-backs dating from 1910-11. McAndrew felt that this class, primarily assigned to Northern Division points, was not as costly to maintain as those already mentioned and should remain in service—a determination that had to be relative considering his comments on the condition of the rest of the O&W's motive power, which was in a state of deferred maintenance. McAndrew indicated that the road was approaching or had reached the "federal limit" on a number of items which came under government inspection. Complicating the situation was the fact that shop forces had been cut because of depressed business, and even those men retained were not working full time.

Conditions did improve between 1938 and 1943, however. The railroad was only tenths of a percentage point below the national average in locomotive availability during that period, while it was spending about one-third less than the average repair costs to keep engines running. After

1941, the 44-tonners were a significant help in maintaining these figures.

The report predated the railroad's bankruptcy by only a short time, but it was used by the bankruptcy trustee and the court to determine which locomotives could be operated at the lowest cost to the railroad and thus were worth repairing and keeping. After Lyford convinced the court that diesels could save even more money, improve service levels and replace a significant number of steam engines, the next question was which model and manufacturer to choose.

Although Electro-Motive Corporation was producing both 600- and 1000-h.p.. switchers, and other manufacturers had similar models, smaller diesels were less expensive, and the General Electric 44-tonner—even at only 380 h.p.—compared favorably with the engines targeted in the retirement report. Those steam engines ranged roughly from 65 to 80 tons but were close to the 44-ton model in tractive effort. However, the diesel's lower weight meant fewer track or structural limitations to restrict their travel or work assignments.

Trustee Lyford seemed to have particular interest making the northern reaches of the rail-

(ABOVE) A rare photo of GE demonstrator unit 12945 shows the locomotive on the O&W in May 1941, possibly at Sidney. The O&W's production units, unlike the demonstrator, would have two sets of steps on each side located at the extreme ends of the walkways.—O&W SOCIETY COLLECTION.

road more profitable, and a survey conducted by Coverdale & Colpitts indicated that this was possible. The loan application for the diesels listed the railroad's primary shippers by volume and location, and many of these customers were on the Northern Division where the 44-tonners could reduce the costs of providing service. Oswego, Arrowhead, Fulton, Sidney and Walton were to be the homes of the O&W's first diesels where they would serve local industries and handle yard work.

The northern terminals had to be supplied with coal, water, lubricants and other items essential for proper maintenance of the assigned steam locomotives. This required clerical accounting as well as company or foreign-line freight cars to haul in the fuel and supplies. At Oneida, and possibly other locations, water required for steam locomotives contained minerals that had to be removed by an expensive treatment process. Such fixed facilities and non-revenue car movements absorbed valuable dollars in maintenance, operation and taxes. In places like Cadosia, Mayfield, Middletown and Sidney,

the facilities were more frequently used by road, yard and local freight engines and thus their existence was more justified. In addition, steam locomotives assigned to outlying points had to make frequent runs into Norwich or Middletown for inspection and repairs. The down time for this work, especially on older-class engines, was significantly greater than that for a diesel.

Five small diesel locomotives wouldn't totally eliminate all of these time and monetary costs on the Northern Division, but they would certainly reduce them. The conclusion: Dieselization could very likely be a successful approach to turning around those parts of the system where profit was marginal or non-existent as long as the work did not overtax the abilities of the small locomotives.

As it turned out, World War II forced the O&W to retain some of the steam power that was to have been scrapped. Nonetheless, several classes mentioned in the motive-power report did disappear in whole or in part over the next few years including most of the I's and I-1's, the remaining S, the U and U-1 classes and many of the V's. Most of the P class soldiered through to the mid-1940's. All of these retired classes had tractive efforts around 30,000 pounds versus 26,400 for the GE's. O&W's intention was to replace a number of well-worn steam locomotives that handled local freight and branchline as well as yard-switching chores. Although management would have liked to have had more diesels to handle such work, the E, L and W classes and the handful of remaining members of the classes listed above were to remain for several more years.

Why did O&W first choose GE? Perhaps the O&W felt that GE had a closer connection to Class I railroads than did other builders—notably Davenport, Whitcomb and Porter—of small diesels, which seemed to wind up more in industrial applications and on shortlines. A more likely reason was that GE was the only locomotive

(RIGHT) The 103 stands in profile circa 1946. Some railroads were said to wax the finish of their new diesels but no entry that records the purchase of finishing wax has been found in the O&W records. The 44 tonners' finish must have been very durable, for after five years of service the locomotives still presented an acceptable appearance.—GE PHOTO, O&W SOCIETY COLLECTION.

The 44 tonners were ideal for reaching the farthest extremes of the railroad's mileage. Trundling along the grass-grown reaches of the Port Jervis and Monticello lines or frightening the wildlife along the rural rights-of-way north of Randallsville, the GE's had occasional need for tools like the rerailing frog and push-pole visible above the trucks. Here the 102 sits at Middletown where self-sufficiency is not as critical. Big league help, in the form of one of the O&W's three 90-ton steam derricks, was only a whistle (or horn) shriek away.—MARV COHEN.

builder that had a sales office in every major city and thus fielded sales staffs that could more aggressively pursue a customer.

Another consideration could have been how much General Electric business was routed over the O&W. GE was a large corporation with diversified manufacturing and shipped substantial quantities of its products by rail. The O&W may have been concerned about alienating a shipper.

General Electric's long history in rail transportation dates from early application of outside-source electrical propulsion (i.e., power through overhead catenary or third rail) for locomotives. When on-board electrical generation began to be explored, GE made many significant discoveries which led to the development of reliable gas-electric motorcars. Later, GE was for many years a partner with American Locomotive Company (Alco) producing electrical components which Alco integrated to its diesel prime movers. GE electrical parts were also found in EMC and other manufacturers' locomotives as well. Having fought hard to maintain a

place in the international diesel locomotive market, GE today has outlasted all of its domestic competitors except EMD, which GE now closely rivals. Although GE was not the first to manufacture a low-weight, low-horsepower unit, it had ample experience in dual prime-mover locomotives. The company had built its first such units in 1933 and the concept proved successful. It had several years to refine the design before production of the 44-ton model began in 1940.

That switcher model was one of several built by GE that appealed to industrial and shortline operators. Although many considered them to be designed for industrial use, the 44-tonners were quite capable of performing Class 1 service where the assignments were carefully analyzed and understood to be within the range of the locomotive's capabilities. With the 44-tonner, GE found a special niche in the locomotive market and proceeded to make the most of it by selling over 300 units. Because of the similarities between the various GE models and also between GE's 44-tonner and competing models of other

Passing a line of dead 0-6-0 steam switchers, a class whose tasks the 44-tonners filled admirably, the 102 rolls south through Middletown Yard. Some may view the L-class engines as the steamers most analogous to the small diesels in both appearance—they are both "center-cab" locomotives—and in function. Early orthochromatic films tends to lose the yellow band and accentuate the red cab emblem in this photograph from February 1947.—JOHN P. AHRENS PHOTO, COURTESY OF RAY BROWN.

Locomotives 101, 104 and 105 had multiple-unit capability, which increased their utility. (ABOVE LEFT) This is the only available photograph of two 44-tonners working in multiple. The 104 and 105 are in tandem at Middletown for a Caterpillar Tractor Co. photographer on June 14, 1949. (ABOVE RIGHT) This view of the 105 shows the m.u. jumper cable that carried electrical signals from the lead unit. A hinged lid covered the m.u. cable receptacle when it was not in use.—CATERPILLAR TRACTOR COMPANY PHOTOS, COURTESY OF STERLING KIMBALL, O&W SOCIETY COLLECTION.

One may ask why a 44-tonner, by design a bidirectional locomotive, needed to be turned as the 101 is doing at Middletown. The answer usually was that it was for the convenience of the engineer. If most of the work was on one side of the locomotive on a particular assignment, he wanted to be on that side for ease in communicating with the ground men.—DON WALLWORTH.

manufacturers, rail historians have often erroneously lumped all these small diesel engines together under the heading of "44-tonners," and the name has become more generic than specific to a single manufacturer.

GE's 44-tonner had an impressive list of intrinsic features that made it very attractive. It offered better visibility in both directions than any steam locomotive; it had equal tracking and operational ability in both directions, did not require a fireman, produced less smoke (a concern of food processors such as Nestle's in Fulton), did not have an open fire (a concern at chemical plants) and, with a weight just slightly more than that of a loaded boxcar, it could run on any dock, trestle or light-rail siding. Further, seldom would time be lost in having to turn a unit nor would turning facilities have to be maintained.

Probably the greatest motivating factor for the 44-tonner's design was the "90,000-pound clause" in the 1937 labor contract with enginemen. This clause permitted railroads to operate

locomotives below that weight without a fireman. It appears GE correctly anticipated the industry's response to the opportunity to cut labor costs and thus received the bulk of mainline railroad orders.

In addition to the labor- and maintenance-saving features and in regard to several fixed-plant requirements previously mentioned, diesels did not require extensive ministrations of a hostler, the emptying of an ashpit, the constant applications of valve oil, and grease guns. When the day's work was done, the engineer could shut the engine off and walk away. Fueling could be handled by a local oil supplier if the railroad didn't want to install its own tank and pump.

Because of these potential savings, GE claimed that the 44-tonner could be operated in switching service at $1.43 per hour and road service at $2.18 per hour compared with $3.28 and $5.34 respectively for a steam locomotive. O&W management figured that the units could pay for themselves out of savings in five years.

The main components of the 44-tonner during that period were a pair of Caterpillar 190-h.p. V-8 D17000 diesel engines. The D17000 was a heavy-duty non-turbocharged industrial engine which was of a four-cycle design with a 5¾-inch bore, 8-inch stroke and a 1,662-cubic-inch displacement. Caterpillar originally had developed the D17000 for a wide variety of stationary purposes, but it was found to have excellent application to railroading. The Caterpillar diesel was the most common prime mover employed by GE, but some earlier and later production runs used Buda, Hercules or Cummins engines with accompanying variations in horsepower.

In the 44-tonner, the two engines were directly connected via flexible-disc couplings to shunt-

wound, direct-current GT555 generators. When starting the locomotive, these generators, powered by batteries, acted as motors to crank the engines. The engines were cooled by thermostatically controlled systems that maintained a water temperature between 160-180 degrees Fahrenheit. Kerosene-fired water heaters (one for each engine) were standard—and welcome equipment where a heated enginehouse was not available.

Four truck-mounted GE 733 traction motors were semi-permanently connected in parallel to the main generator. They engaged the axles with double-reduction spur gearing enclosed in single-sealed housings. The wheels were 33 inches in diameter. Not all small diesels had traction motors on all axles. Truck design told whether a locomotive was built for industrial/shortline or mainline railroad work. Industrial units frequently had one axle powered on each truck and used side rods or a chain-drive to propel the other. For heavier railroad work, all axles had traction motors.

Both the locomotive frame and the trucks were of welded fabrication with the hoods and cab formed of shaped and arc-welded sheet steel. The fuel tank had a 250-gallon capacity, and the locomotive's total loaded weight was close to 89,000 pounds. A pair of air-cooled, belt-driven compressors provided a reservoir pressure of 140 pounds for the brake system. A 44-tonner had a maximum speed of 35 m.p.h., and it could negotiate a 125-foot-radius curve when coupled to a freight car.

One of the best features of the small units was their short "load" time. That is, little time elapsed between pulling out the throttle, revving up the diesel and the generator and getting motion at the wheels. One can imagine the reaction of old engineers who had spent their lifetimes horsing Johnson bars and throttle levers back and forth in steam switching service. Two stubby, easy-to-move levers sticking out of the control stand did the same jobs on the 44-tonners.

If those same engineers had worked on Camelbacks, the high center cab of the 44-tonner might have provided them with some reminder of their former surroundings—minus the hot boiler and maze of piping and valves, of course. The 44-tonner's high cab not only provided excellent visibility but also permitted the battery compartment to fit between the cab floor and frame. On the other hand, good visibility did not always make up for the lack of a fireman. When necessary, the ground crew had to be sure there was someone on the engineer's side of the cars to pass signals to the cab during switching.

GE's production of the 44-tonner continued through to 1956. Production runs, particularly one of this length, can usually be broken down into phases which are characterized by changes in components, design and fabrication techniques which, in turn, may alter external appearances. Although these phases may not be officially recognized by the manufacturer, more astute members of the rail history corps have completed painstaking research to confirm their occurrence. (The leader in this area is *Extra 2200 South*, The Locomotive Newsmagazine. Those issues produced under the editorship of the Dover family have been extensively used for this book.)

The O&W's 44-tonners

After the trustee received the court's permission to look into diesel operations, the judge agreed that, "The railroad needed to acquire the locomotives as the result of a study which definitely established that such acquisition will enable the road to perform switching services at five points with marked economy in operating costs."

Arrangements were made with General Electric to have their 44-ton demonstrator, No. 12945, visit the property in May 1941. The locomotive was picked up from the Lehigh Valley at Coxton, Pa., on May 5 and moved to Oswego, N.Y. After a day's assignment there, it moved south through the state to work a day or two at Fulton, and then on to Norwich, Sidney, Walton and Middletown and finally Weehawken, N.J. On May 23 it was delivered to the D&H at Jermyn Transfer, Pa. The 12945's tour was deemed successful, and with the approval of the court, the railroad placed its order.

Unfortunately, the railroad had failed to arrange financing arrangements with either New York City banks or dealers in equipment trusts. For alternative financing, Trustee Lyford applied for and received Interstate Commerce Commission permission to apply to the Reconstruction Finance Corporation for assistance. Lyford had earlier worked for the RFC as an investigator of rail properties seeking the agency's assistance, so no doubt his knowledge of its functions and methods of operation was an asset to the O&W's application for aid.

The railroad sold $162,000 of equipment trust certificates to the RFC. This money was deposit-

Some photographic evidence seems to indicate that the O&W's first diesels were assigned, by number, to specific locations. This may have been true during the steam years but probably ended with the arrival of the NW2's, if not earlier. In this scene, the 104 works at Sidney where a good deal of its time would have been spent pulling the D&H interchange—RAY BROWN COLLECTION.

ed with the Orange County Trust Company, which served as trustee for the New York, Ontario & Western Equipment Trust of 1941. The railroad was to pay biannual installments to the trust company, which was the legal owner and lessor of the locomotives through the final payment due Nov. 1, 1951. The total GE order cost $181,000 for which $162,900 was raised by the certificates and $18,100 was paid in cash by the railroad. As events would later prove, the Equipment Trust of 1941 would be the only one of three such trusts that the railroad would pay in full.

Locomotives 101, 102 and 103 were delivered on Dec. 17, 1941. The 104 arrived on Jan. 13, 1942, and the 105 came in August. O&W's 44-tonners were Phase Ic units and differed from earlier and subsequent 44-tonner production by way of the following features: side rather than end radiator shutters, engine access doors that opened toward the ends, three hinged louvers at the top of each of these doors, and relatively plain hood ends.

The units cost $35,000 each and they were given a full paragraph mention in O&W's annual report for 1941. The paragraph closed with, "It is expected by the Trustee of the property that substantial economies in operation will be effected by the acquisition of these engines." Originally, the company had expected to save $30,000 annually with the new diesels.

Thomas B. Girard, superintendent of car service, was assigned to evaluate the new locomotives and develop figures for actual savings. Based upon a unit cost of $36,000 and figuring each locomotive's life span to be 25 years, Girard indicated that the GE's were costing the railroad 27 cents per hour. During their first five months of operation, they worked 90 percent of the time and produced a savings of $2.965 per day over equivalent steam operations. Following the arrival of the 105 in August 1942, the savings approached an annual figure of $130,000—more than four times the best estimates of 1941. The officials were greatly impressed.

GE offered several standard paint schemes on its 44-tonners, and the O&W had selected one that was both attractive in design and regal in color choice. The carbody, fuel tank skirts and cab were finished in maroon (at least one O&W communication referred to Tuscan red) which extended slightly above a two-inch wide horizontal silver stripe that passed just below the cab windows and wrapped around the entire unit. The area above the maroon was painted black. Four additional silver stripes, four inches wide and trimmed in black, wrapped around the ends and onto the sides over the radiator shutters. A 28-inch diameter O&W logo, 12-inch numerals and three-inch company initials, all in silver, decorated the cab sides. To the right of the headlight on each end were three-inch silver numerals. Since the 44-tonners were born during the period that the road's maroon-and-orange *Mountaineer Limited* was in operation, it's conceivable that the

Mountaineer livery bore some influence on the colors selected for O&W's first diesels. In fact, the GE painting specifications list "NYO&W standard maroon" for finishing. The livery would be relatively short-lived. A memo from Superintendent of Motive Power I. R. Pease dated Oct. 8, 1945, indicated that the 44-tonners were to be repainted in the same colors of the new EMD units.

In 1947, a Northern Division road foreman made a list of inspection items for which a fireman on a 44-tonner was responsible. It is not known if firemen had by then been placed on all 44-tonners, or only on certain jobs that might have required a second man in the cab, or when this practice was instituted. Whatever the cause, this additional expense reduced the number of reasons for employing these locomotives after the NW2's arrived. Although GE indicated that the units were good for 35 m.p.h., the O&W put out bulletin orders that they were not to exceed 25 m.p.h.

The m.u. capability of diesel power was one of its most significant advantages over steam power. It allowed for the transmission of electrical signals from the control stand of the lead locomotive to be passed back to following units via jumper or m.u. cables. In December 1948, the 101 and 104 received multiple-unit (m.u.) wiring, connections and controls at a cost of approximately $3,000 per unit; the 105 was likewise equipped in September 1949. Now, two—or possibly all three—of the 44-tonners so equipped could be controlled by one engineer for handling heavier trains.

There is evidence, albeit non-conclusive, that the m.u. systems were applied to the 44-tonners when they were reassigned to the mountainous Southern Division and based at Middletown. Unlike operation in the flat north country, the 44-tonners lost much of their pulling ability when they encountered grades.

There was a chance that the 44-tonners were proving at least a trifle light for some purposes as the company tried to further consolidate operations by cutting the number of crews in switching, local, passenger and through service. In 1948, 21 EMD NW2 switchers arrived. For a few years, the GE's served concurrently with these larger switchers, which allowed ample time for

comparison. Apparently, the NW2's were able to perform any task the smaller diesels handled—even on light track—although they were almost three times the weight and required a fireman.

Why did the O&W get rid of its 44-tonners in 1950-51? We can only surmise. Little at this time is known about the operational and managerial philosophies—and idiosyncrasies—of O&W officers and motive-power managers in regard to locomotive manufacturers, specific models, service levels and such, for all of these considerations had much to do with decisions relating to motive power. (Divergent views can be seen today with one road relying on a pair of GE six-axle units to perform the same service to which another road assigns three EMD four-axle diesels.)

Perhaps one reason O&W sold the GE's after only a decade was that the EMD-built FT's, NW2's and F3's shared many interchangeable parts, but the GE's required their own supply of components. Dealing with a single manufacturer/supplier eased inventory procedures and expenses, and since there were now more EMD's on the property than GE's, the 44-tonners had become the "odd men out." But the most obvious thought is that they were loan collateral and could not be sold until the equipment trust was paid off (or most of the principal was paid and any remaining balance could be met by sale).

Whatever the reason for their somewhat early departure, the diminutive GE's gave the O&W an opportunity to "test the waters" so far as diesels were concerned. They proved that internal-combustion motive power saved money and could do so in a reliable manner.

"Vest-pocket switchers," *Trains* Magazine called the 44-tonners many years ago, and the analogy was a good one up to a point. Relative to what was to come, they were small in size but definitely not in terms of endurance. After a decade of working for the O&W, the 44-tonners went on to serve other properties. They outlasted the railroad for which they were built and, with few exceptions, all the larger diesels that came to the O&W after them. Four of the GE's managed to reach the half-century mark, and three of them exist at the time of this writing. That speaks highly about the design and quality of General Electric locomotives.

Very few curves broke the angular appearances of a 44 tonner. From any perspective it was a highly functional design produced at a price to make it an attractive tool for the economy-minded railroad. Clear lines-of-sight between the cab and ground crews are evident in this end view of No. 103. Also note the variety of grab irons and railing for the convenience of brakemen.—O&W SOCIETY COLLECTION.

4/The Electro-Motive FT's

Steam locomotives generally were custom-designed machines. A railroad's engineering staff and mechanical officers had a great deal of input on the design of the locomotives that moved the freight and passengers over their line. And although each railroad was interested in what its neighbors were doing in motive-power design and application, each regarded itself as having unique characteristics and beliefs in the efficacy of specific steam-locomotive designs and appliances. The United States Railroad Administration (USRA) designs of the late World War I era were the closest ideas to a steam-locomotive consensus that America's railroads achieved in this century, but they weren't at all close to the motive-power standardization that was approaching. The idea of a universal, internal-combustion locomotive that, with minor changes, could meet all operational mainline needs, was essentially inconceivable. Diesel locomotive manufacturers did not think so.

In the 1930's, several such manufacturers changed much of that thinking by producing mainline locomotives in large numbers in the same manner as automobile manufacturers built cars: on a production line basis using standard-ized parts and assembly procedures. By the late 1930's, Electro-Motive Corporation had established itself as a leader in the field. In large measure the company was successful because it had not been tied to a tradition of steam-locomotive construction. It had achieved successes in the development of electro-motive propulsion largely because it did not have an administration or floor staff with a collective mind-set formed by years of steam-locomotive design, assembly and operation. Also it did not have the "split personality" of steam builders who had diesel divisions. However, selling its new ideas to railroaders was another matter.

The 17th Century Enlightenment physicist Isaac Newton explained inertia by saying that an object at rest or in motion will remain at rest or in motion unless acted upon by an outside force. The same could be said of in-place technologies. The entrenched thinking about motive power would only be changed after a great deal of "force" (in the form of enlightenment on the subject of dieselization) had been applied. A steam locomotive, in spite of its inherent limitations, was a tried, true and familiar machine.

Steam locomotion was produced by heavy,

hot, tough, metal fireboxes, boilers, wheels and rods that assailed the senses with the inferno of their energy source and the fury of their external workings. Many of its repairs could be made with a sledge hammer and other simple tools by a man with a minimum of formal education. The parts were bulky, their mechanical relationships were obvious and seen as anthropomorphic. Now, along came the diesel locomotive with its accompanying lab-coated technician holding a manual in one hand, a screwdriver in the other, making adjustments in a cabinet on a machine that—outwardly anyway—hardly did more in motion than it did while it was standing still.

Today, diesel-electric technology makes perfect sense to most of us, but in the 1930's, trying to explain how invisible moving electrons were going to power an 8,000-ton train over a mountain range was really not much different from Columbus explaining that he could reach the east by sailing west.

It is difficult for a current generation to look at an accepted technology and understand why it did not replace a preceding technology more quickly. An historian of technology, Lewis Mumford, said, "inventions are often patented long before they can be practicably used, and, on the other hand, they are often ready for use long before industrial enterprisers are willing to take advantage of them." Many institutions, agencies and industries—especially the railroad industry—were steeped in tradition and custom. Evolution, both technological and psychological, is usually a slow process and the promoters of

change require patience, perseverance and powers of persuasion.

An excellent example of this can be seen in the volume of correspondence between NYO&W officials as they discussed how their diesel units should be numbered when operated in multiple-unit configurations. At first, they could not get away from the idea of treating fixed sets of two-, three- and four-unit locomotives as a single locomotive having a single number. Complex numbering schemes were developed for each set just as each class of steam locomotives had it own number series. Eventually—probably with the suggestions of EMD people and Interstate Commerce Commission edicts—they broke through the barrier of "past practice thinking," accepted the wonderful simplicity and adaptability of the unit concept, established an elementary numbering scheme and entered the diesel era.

Despite awareness of Electro Motive's and other manufacturers' earlier successes with railcars, switching locomotives and passenger diesels in the 1930's, it was a general belief within the rail industry that freight hauling would remain the job of steam locomotives for a long time to come. EMC and other diesel builders took this as a challenge. The company had gained a tremendous amount of knowledge regarding railroad operation and locomotive manufacturing since its inception in 1922 and, with the financial and engineering backing of General Motors Corporation when it became a division of that company in 1930, it looked for a way to

(FACING PAGE) In a scene that bespeaks industrial might, an impressive A-B-B-A set of clean O&W FT's sweeps over D&H's main line, a portion of the downtown area of Carbondale, Pa., and the Lackawanna River in September 1947. Postwar euphoria is just setting in, and a nearly dieselized O&W gambles its future on internal combustion power. In steam days, local residents were accustomed to seeing pusher locomotives behind the long freights since the grade between Mayfield Yard and the crest at Poyntelle rose 70 feet per mile. Diesel-powered trains seldom required helpers.—JOHN PICKETT. (ABOVE LEFT) Fresh from the assembly line, O&W FT's have their first portraits taken at LaGrange, Ill. Within a few days, they will be heading east to take up the task of bringing a financially anemic railroad back to health.—ELECTRO-MOTIVE DIVISION, GENERAL MOTORS CORP.

apply its expanded technology to pulling freight trains.

General Motors had been very interested in the diesel engine and decided that its promise justified the corporation's entry into the manufacture of diesel locomotives. Instead of creating a new division from scratch, it put one together using existing companies as components. After GM purchased the Winton engine company in June 1930, it bought Electro-Motive Engineering Corporation in December 1930 and put the two together as a subsidiary company, Electro-Motive Corporation. In 1935, encouraged by its sales of passenger and switching locomotives, GM gave a go-ahead for the new division to begin construction of a diesel-locomotive assembly

plant in LaGrange, Ill. Since its inception, EMC had subcontracted the assembly of its units and purchased practically all the components from various manufacturers. This practice would soon change dramatically.

The Depression would not seem to be an auspicious time to build a new locomotive assembly facility since many potential customers were having serious financial problems. However, it was thought that railroads facing severe economic restrictions might be better customers for money-saving diesels than healthy roads. GM was correct in this thinking, and the decision to produce lightweight, high-speed locomotives engineered, manufactured and marketed using automobile industry methods was to pay great dividends.

Highly prominent among EMC's early engineering staff was Richard M. Dilworth, who joined the company in 1926 and became its chief engineer. Dilworth could be considered one of several claimants to the title, "Father of the road freight diesel." Dilworth brought many successful concepts to the design of diesel locomotives and was influential in Electro-Motive decision-making for several decades. He was instrumental in EMC's development of its own generators and traction motors—the axle-mounted electric motors that actually turned the wheels.

The model 567 diesel prime mover (so named because of its 567-cubic-inch displacement per cylinder) developed by Eugene Kettering and his staff would drive "in-house"-developed electrical gear which, along with other EMC-produced components, were to prove successful and durable. Other individuals contributed a host of smaller but equally important innovations and production techniques such as welded construction of frames and prime mover subassemblies. Mechanical engineer Martin Blomberg serves as an example. In 1935, Blomberg came to EMC from Pullman-Standard and developed a new three-axle truck that made its debut in 1937. Based upon its success, he then created a two-axle version that would support an entire line of new locomotives.

Now in possession of the components and their manufacturing means, EMC set out to build a diesel that would have mainline, freight-

(BELOW) Painted dark green with yellow striping, 194-foot long FT demonstrator set No. 103 sits in an unidentified locomotive terminal where it is the object of speculation, wonder, suspicion and perhaps even disdain. If asked to bet on the existence of either the coaling tower or the diesels ten years hence, most of the money would probably have been on the coaling tower. (FACING PAGE INSET) The 103's control stands.—TWO PHOTOS, EMD, COURTESY CARSTENS PUBLICATIONS. (LEFT) Where steam locomotive boilers were once hoisted aloft, diesel locomotive trucks are now dropped. The cost of dieselization included the modification of shop and repair facilities.—ED CRIST COLLECTION.

Richard M. Dilworth

THE MAN WHO HAD SO MUCH TO DO the development of the F unit was unpretentious, crusty and not one to respect railroad tradition. Richard M. Dilworth was born in the Pacific Northwest in 1885 before the frontier was more than just memory. He received little formal schooling and left home at an early age. With an interest and talent for things mechanical, he wandered into a variety of jobs involving machine shop work and the use of metal-working tools. Other early jobs included that of a circus roustabout and crewing on a windjammer in the South American trade. His earliest railroad-related work was the delivering of a logging locomotive from Pennsylvania to Oregon. A few years in the Navy provided some discipline and a knowledge of electricity.

By his mid-twenties, he was a competent electrician for his time and he found employment with General Electric where he was eventually drawn into their gas-electric railcar program. Delivering these cars to various railroads taught him the many facets of the rail industry. Dilworth was later assigned to GE's Erie, Pa., works where he came in contact with the legendary Dr. Herman Lemp who was in charge of diesel development for GE. After the company dropped its railcar interest, Dilworth went over to the turbine division.

In the mid-1920's, he met H. L. Hamilton who was reviving the interest in rail cars and was putting together Electro-Motive Corporation, a company that would be noted for innovative and iconoclastic engine designs that eventually carried over into diesel locomotives. Following General Motors' acquisition of EMC in 1930, Dilworth got involved in the Zephyr project being conducted for the Burlington. After that was completed he went on to the production of the boxy, two-unit passenger diesel that was to release the diesel locomotive from the fixed passenger consist designs of which the Zephyr was an example. The units were tested on the B&O where Col. George Emerson, B&O's motive-power chief and a rail industry spokesman asked why General Motors was willing to fund the diesel project instead of getting railroads involved. The reply from Dilworth, with his typical directness was, "So you fellows won't tell us how to build it."

EMC wanted to develop a product that, with only minor modifications, could be sold to practically all railroads, not something that reflected the pet theories and practices of individual mechanical officers. Dilworth in

particular did not want "a horse designed by a committee" (one definition of a camel). The engines were successful enough to encourage GM to invest in a production facility for its EMC subsidiary where it could develop and manufacture passenger diesels and switching locomotives that provided the speed and economy that railroads were looking for.

Continued development under Dilworth's leadership led to a successful freight diesel, the FT, that, fortunately, came in time to aid the country during World War II. More than twenty railroads bought the road freight diesel, pronounced it highly successful, and planned to add more to their rosters as soon as possible. Despite the triumph, there was still strong resistance to diesels for many years and one road (probably the Union Pacific) believed internal combustion could never equal its "Big Boy." Dilworth's response was that if the road would try EMD's four-unit freight locomotive, it would see the diesel "push your Big Boy far back into Lionel's window with the rest of the toys, and no one would ever talk about it again."

Once the dieselization of America's railroads was truly underway, Dilworth was placed in charge of GM's Advanced Engineering Department where he developed additional concepts for both American and foreign railroads. In appreciation for such a contribution to "the land down under," an Australian took poet Rudyard Kipling's "On the Road to Mandalay" and created the following tribute. (O&W enthusiasts may wish to substitute "old North Bay" for Santa Fe.).

On the road to Santa Fe
Where the flying diesels play,
Rootin', tootin' on their whistles
As they claim the right of way,

Hear them screaming for the crossing
Dashing past the old steam pots.
Stand aside, you puffing billies,
We can't wait while you get hot!

Watch them ride into the depot,
Rolling down with conscious pride.
We're Dick Dilworth's pups they holler,
He's the man who made us stride!

—R.M.

hauling ability. Experience gained from earlier work with passenger units was heavily drawn upon. This was obvious in the freight unit's structural arrangement and general appearance. The 1930's marked the first decade of the science of industrial design. Men such as Henry Dreyfuss, Norman Bel Geddes, Otto Kuhler, Raymond Loewy and Walter Dorwin Teague joined mechanical engineers in many successful efforts which proved utility, beauty and elegance could be combined in forms that excited the public and revitalized depressed industries as well as a depressed nation.

A high point in this movement was the artistic direction in which EMC locomotive designs were channeled. The beautiful, streamlined pas-

senger diesels built for Santa Fe, Rock Island, Baltimore & Ohio and other lines are yet recalled as examples of how science and technology could lead the world out of a stark, dreary era. The early boxy carbodies of road units had been replaced by the Art Deco-influenced streamlined shapes that were applied to objects as divergent as locomotives and home vacuum cleaners. Such styling was not only aestheticly pleasing, but also practical. It gave enginemen greater protection and better visibility. Moving the engine crew up and back from the front eliminated the mesmerizing effect of ties and rail flashing under the pilot, and the rounded, sloped nose better deflected objects in the locomotive's path and also made the locomotive better able to cope with

With a James Strates Show circus train in tow, four FT's tiptoe along the grassy right-of-way of the Utica Branch in the mid-1950's. The train was delivered to the O&W by New York Central at Utica. A special move like this would have plenty of attention from a railroad's supervisors, and it is a certainty that a road foreman, trainmaster or other high official is in 807's cab. Planning for such moves went on well in advance, and if the O&W did not meet the planned schedule, it would have to pay for the missed performance.—BOB MORGAN.

(ABOVE) Train MT-9, once the northbound distributor of empty milk cars, is stopped at Summitville, N.Y, on July 11, 1951. By this time, the run had become a local road freight that set out and picked up cars at major points on the line. The baggage-RPO (Railway Post Office) car and baggage car suggest that O&W still had a U.S. Mail contract and still handled l.c.l. (less-than-carload) freight. The Railway Express Agency truck undoubtedly was awaiting l.c.l. shipments.—KEN BEALER COLLECTION.

heavy snow conditions. The general design was to remain in production into the 1960's.

EMC shortened the length of the passenger locomotive nose design for the freight unit, bringing the coupler closer to the truck bolster to permit locomotive movement through tighter curves. The foreshortening blunted the stream-lined appearance and gave rise to the "bulldog nose" that became a distinct property of EMD cab units.

When EMC abandoned the boxcab styling of its first passenger diesels, it became necessary to position the prime mover and generator farther back into the car body. Previously, this heavy machinery had rested on a thick frame which in turn sat on the bolsters. With the streamlined passenger diesels, a new system was needed and it came from an old idea. A bridge truss was employed to rest on the bolsters and support the engine and generator by chords connected to the locomotive floor by vertical and diagonal frame members. A surprising feature of the carbody construction was the use of 3/8-inch laminated wood panels for the sides; the wood was covered by and bonded to galvanized steel sheets. These panels were held in place by battens but were not penetrated by fasteners. The framing of the curved front end was covered with formed sections of 12-gauge steel which were welded to frame members.

The freight diesel was to be known as the FT model, the F representing Freight and the T,

(ABOVE) FT 601—the Standard Oil Development set—gleams in the sun at Electro-Motive Division's LaGrange plant in suburban Chicago in 1945.—EMD
PHOTO. *(RIGHT) Pages from the EMD FT instruction manual included this overall arrangement diagram of an A-B set of FT's, showing both external and internal principal components.—*
AUTHOR'S COLLECTION.

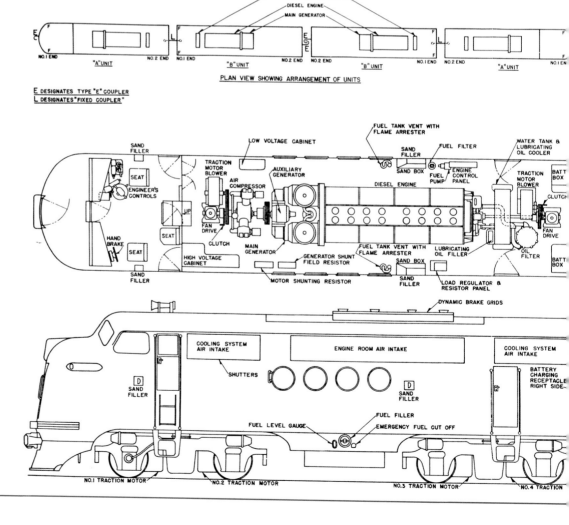

Twenty-seven hundred horsepower. Dilworth actually planned and produced a pair of locomotives, each composed of two 1350-h.p. "sections" (the term "unit" came later) that were less than 50 feet long and rode on 40-inch wheels. To accommodate a coupler and heavy draftgear that had been designed and built for steam locomotive tenders, the front truck of the A section and the rear truck of the B section were located farther back under the frame than they would be in later F-series models. (The same frame was used for both A and B sections and they were joined "back-to-back." Advances in draft-gear design would reduce the size and weight of coupler mountings so that trucks of later models would be equally distant from the ends.)

Each FT pair was composed of a control cab A section semi-permanently coupled to a B section by means of a drawbar. The B section was not intended to operate separately and in fact it was impossible to do so initially. (Several railroads later modified or asked Electro-Motive to build B units that had their own batteries and controls for independent movement in locomotive service areas.) A pair of two-section locomotives could be coupled to make a "single" 5400-h.p. locomotive which had a hauling ability that was at least equal to the largest 4-8-4 steam locomotive of the day. Although the idea of building "blocks" or units of horsepower to make a locomotive was not new, most railroads, especially those that had no experience with diesel or electric locomotives, were skeptical of the concept.

EMC began assembly of the FT early in 1939 and by November of the same year the first four-unit diesel, numbered 103, came through the shop doors and was given its initial testing on the nearby Baltimore & Ohio Chicago Terminal Railroad. After a basic shake down, the locomotive returned to EMC for minor adjustments and later in the month began an epic 84,000-mile, ten-month, 20-railroad demonstration tour across the U.S. On several occasions, the pairs were separated to demonstrate as two 2700-h.p. locomotives. The tour proved that diesels could move freight tonnage equally as well, and frequently better, than steam power and could do it more efficiently.

The success of the tour was highly publicized by EMC in the railroad trade press with full

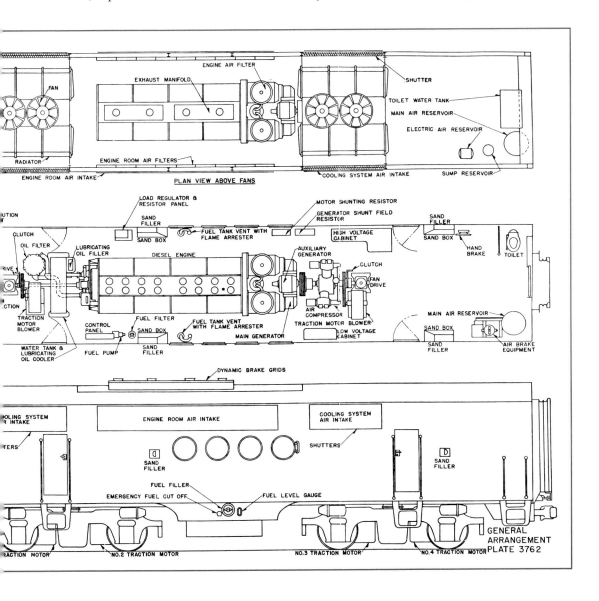

51

(ABOVE) In the final season of passenger service, FT's lead No. 2 near Roscoe on Sept. 7, 1953. The consist is made up largely of NYC coaches. Although the FT's did not have steam generators for train heating, they were often used on passenger runs during the summer season when heating was unnecessary.—DAVID CONNOR. (RIGHT) A low sun and the threat of more snow greets FT's on a winter morning in Middletown. Before the short day is over, these locomotives may be scores of miles distant, and the front end plastered with snow with the exception of two arcs cleared by windshield wipers.—MARV COHEN.

color publicity and sales publications. Booklets containing specifications and statistical data were circulated among motive-power departments and upper management. Roads that did not host the 103 eventually sent representatives to the roads that were buying the new diesels to get a firsthand impression. The first railroad to order the FT was the Santa Fe in October 1940, and it would eventually have the largest roster of the model.

At the heart of the FT was the prime-mover: the 16-cylinder, model 567, two-cycle, 45-degree "V" diesel engine that took General Motors 18 months of intensive effort to develop. It had three key design elements: suitability for mass production, reliability and easy maintenance.

Unlike the earlier Winton engines, which were designed for a number of different applications, the 567 was specifically produced for locomotives. The 16-cylinder version was the largest of three 567 designs for railroad use; eight- and 12-cylinder versions used many parts interchangeably with the 16-cylinder model. (As it turned out, World War II pressure led to other, non-railroad applications for the 567 series since time could not be spared for new designs, and the government strongly encouraged standardization to reduce inventories.) The engine was directly coupled to an EMC model D8, 600-volt main generator which fed electricity to a d.c. series-wound traction motor on each of the four axles.

Two sets of radiators were mounted against

the ceiling at each end of the diesel engine. This left clearance for pulling out cylinder liners or performing other work in the tight quarters of the engineroom. Cooling air was taken in through the two manually controlled, shuttered openings located near the roof on both sides of the unit. The unshuttered long intake above the four portholes was for engine, compressor and traction-motor cooling air. The heated cooling-system air was exhausted through a pair of roof-mounted fans over the two sets of radiators.

These fans were mechanically driven by a system of shafts, belts, clutches and gears that must have reminded an observer of an old belt-driven, wood-working shop. The same mechanical system also powered the traction motor blowers over both trucks. This complicated arrangement replaced electrically powered auxiliary systems used for the same functions on earlier diesels, permitting EMC to cut the purchase price of the new diesel. Nonetheless, the many bearing surfaces of the system's shafts, pulleys and gears had to be inspected for proper alignment, tension and lubrication—and for wear. The system became a weak point in the FT, and subsequent locomotive models would return to

electrically driven radiator fans and traction-motor blowers.

The FT required a good deal more decision-making from the engineer and fireman than diesels of today. In fact, it was necessary for the fireman to periodically leave the cab and move through the units to monitor the locomotive innards, notably the cooling systems. A bell system connected all units and allowed communication between the engineer and fireman when the latter was out of the cab. Two significant improvements which appeared in models subsequent to the FT were automatic engine-cooling-system temperature control and automatic transition.

Engine-cooling water temperature had to be kept within a 15-degree range of 165 degrees Fahrenheit. Temperature was controlled by manual operation of the radiator shutters. Under very cold conditions, the clutch controlling the forward radiator fans was disengaged and the shutters closed. An alarm bell and warning light indicated a cooling water temperature in excess of 200 degrees.

Transition is the process of changing electrical connections between the generator and the individual traction motors so that the greatest

Tom J. Donahue, a Connecticut resident and New Haven enthusiast, visited the extreme western end of his favorite road at Campbell Hall and happened to catch O&W trains in the process. FT set 801 leads train BC-3 off the Maybrook connection, onto the O&W main and across Erie's Pine Island-Montgomery (N.Y.) branch. From the same location one also could have watched Lehigh & New England, NYC and Erie trains.—T. J. Donahue.

pulling power is achieved for a particular speed and load range. Transition had to be done manually on an FT and required good judgment on the part of the engineer. The transition lever had four positions relative to the four electrical connection arrangements: series-parallel, series-parallel-shunt, parallel and parallel-shunt. Transition was made by watching the dial on a transition meter—actually an ammeter—and shifting a short handle on the control stand toward the left in response to the reading. Failure to make proper transition could cause the main generator to "flash" (arc) and create an electrical failure. Moving the handle to the right controlled the dynamic braking when that system was in use.

Regenerative or dynamic brakes had been used on straight-electric locomotives for many years, and mountain-climbing electrified lines like the Milwaukee Road, Virginian, Great Northern and a number of smaller lines used the brake to good advantage. Essentially, the activation of dynamic braking reverses the function of a locomotive's traction motors on a downgrade by changing them into generators. In dynamic-brake mode, the current flow from the main generator through the traction-motor fields is increased ("excited"), and the armature circuits try to generate more power, making them harder to turn and requiring more torque input from the wheels and axles. This in turn produces a drag or retarding effect in each locomotive, thus slowing the train.

As generators, of course, traction motors also produce electricity. On direct-current straight-electric locomotives, current produced through the dynamic-braking procedure was simply fed back into the catenary wire (thus the term "regenerative braking") for resale to the electric company or for other railroad use, such as to assist upgrade trains elsewhere on the line. On diesel-electrics, that current would have nowhere to go and would turn into excessive heat and burn up the traction motor.

A European engineer believed that dynamic braking could also be applied to diesel-electric locomotives if an alternate method could be found for disposing generated current. EMC picked up the idea and applied it to the FT, calling it the "grid-type electric holding brake." The 103 demonstrator set was not equipped with dynamic brakes, but they did appear early in regular production. FT's equipped with dynamic brakes simply dispersed the generated current ("load") as heat through air-cooled resistance grids located on the roof.

Through a "loop" circuit, the batteries of the lead unit of an A-B FT set were used to mildly excite the main generator of each unit to cause them to excite the fields of their respective traction motors. A rheostat-type of control, operated by the dynamic brake lever, created variation in braking power. Early production FT's only had a two-position dynamic brake—medium and full. As dynamic-brake technology advanced through the 1950's and 1960's, the control circuitry became much more sophisticated providing engine crews with much more precise control of even large multiple-unit locomotive sets.

Used in combination with the air brake, dynamic braking helped keep a train's speed in check, making for safer and smoother train handling as well as reducing brake-shoe and wheel wear on cars and locomotives. It also reduced or eliminated lost time spent in cooling wheels and turning down retainer valves after a long or steep descent. An automobile driver may think of dynamic braking as analogous to putting a vehicle in low gear while descending a hill.

Although the dynamic brake did hold down train speed on a descending grade, it could not

The 803 and its mates begin a northbound trip from Middletown to Mayfield Yard near Scranton. In the engineer's and conductor's possession are Form 19 orders that direct "Engine 803 run Extra Middletown to . . ." and probably indicates a meet point or a location short of other train movement or activity that will require the dispatcher to monitor the 803's progress. Clearly visible in this "down-on" view are the dynamic brakes' boxy air intakes and heated-air exhaust louvers which surround the four exhaust stacks on each unit's roof. This time- and equipment-saving feature will first get its use on this trip on the downgrade between Shawangunk Kill and Fair Oaks, not far north of Middletown.—JIM SHAUGHNESSY.

stop the train. As the train and locomotive slowed, the traction motors' generating ability diminished because the wheels and their rotating armatures were making fewer revolutions, thus generating less retarding force. When the dynamic brake was in use, the fireman was expected to frequently check the system in each unit to see that the grid cooling fans were operating properly.

O&W's FT's

The New York, Ontario & Western was the last railroad to place a first order for FT's. After the O&W order, Great Northern, Rock Island and Milwaukee Road reordered and received additional units before FT production ended in November 1945. As a result of its late order, the O&W received units that incorporated many refinements that had resulted from the experience EMD had gained over four years of FT production and operation. One of these improvements

(TOP) The 807 arrives in Cadosia from the north on July 8, 1954, with a brakeman ready to handle the switches. A wooden baggage car in non-revenue service is the first head car. (ABOVE) After dropping the train, the units pulled up to the station where the crew signed off duty. Note the red square on the fuel tank skirt, which marks the emergency fuel shut off. This was to be pulled in the event of an accident to prevent fuel spill and fire hazard. (RIGHT) Its throttle notched down to prevent arcing when the commutator brushes bounce, 808 hammers the diamonds on D&H's Susquehanna Division at GX Tower. Moments earlier, the train had departed Sidney, N.Y., where interchange and local cars had been set out for an assigned NW2 to deliver. Twilight will deepen over the remaining 25 miles of the run into the division point of Norwich. In the days of steam, a helper would have coupled to the rear of the train to assist on the 12-mile grade up to Guilford Summit. Unlike the O&W's right-angle imposition on the terrain, the D&H followed the Susquehanna River through Sidney and did not require a permanent steam helper base in this region.—ALL PHOTOS, DAVID CONNOR.

was a better 567 engine, the 567-A which was introduced in 1943 and remained in production until the final FT left EMD.

Two additional improvements involved the dynamic-brake system, which EMD strongly recommended that the railroad include in its choice of options. The earlier version of this braking system had a limited operating range: 20 mph or less. The refined system, which utilized a rheostat instead of an on/off switch, permitted a wider operating range—9-30 mph. The second refinement involved resistor-grid cooling. Initially, air for cooling these grids was drawn in through square, screened openings that were flush with the roof and located fore and aft of the grid housings and in line with the exhaust stacks and radiators—hardly the best place to find cool air. EMD improved the intake arrangement by laterally mounting a pair of air-intake boxes at the front and back ends of the resistor grid boxes. At the ends of each box, out of line of ra-

diator heat and exhaust gases, were screen-covered air intakes through which air could be drawn by "squirrel cage" fans. Ducting brought this air to the resistor grids. This system appears on later production FT's which included the O&W units.

Although the O&W did not host the 103 demonstration set, the trustee and his staff studied and kept abreast of diesel-locomotive developments. The author recalls conversations held many years ago with engineers Elwin Mumford, Oscar Bennett and Road Foreman Bill Fleming about visits they and other O&W men made to the Boston & Maine to ride its FT's and report on diesel performance.

B&M received their FT's in 1943; neighboring Erie and New York Central got their FT's in 1944 and provided an even closer opportunity for operational and mechanical study. All findings were brought back to Middletown for discussion. The formal dieselization study initiated by

(LEFT) Locomotive 804 pulls into New Haven's receiving yard at Maybrook where the train will be classified for New England destinations. If a return train is ready, the O&W men will change ends on the locomotive, head for the westbound departure yard, wait for the NH to move their caboose over and then head for Middletown.—DON WALLWORTH

(RIGHT) New Haven's black-and-orange road-switchers and green-and-yellow Alco FA's host O&W F's at the Maybrook engine terminal. With a little luck, a visitor here could see locomotives of L&HR, Erie, NH and O&W.—GUY TWADDELL PHOTO, AUTHOR'S COLLECTION. (BELOW) In the spring of 1955, northbound 808 just out of Maybrook is about to cross the Erie at Campbell Hall.—COURTESY OF DEPOT ATTIC AND JOE BUX.

the trustee in 1943 or 1944 brought EMD into the picture, and EMD no doubt felt that turning the O&W around financially through dieselization would be powerful advertising.

The many reports, studies, visits and conferences certainly laid a foundation for O&W dieselization, but nothing would have been a substitute for a firsthand experience with an FT locomotive. One might think that O&W would have approached Erie, B&M or other FT operators to lease a set for testing purposes, but so far as is known, no FT rode O&W rails before 1945, and the reason was probably the war. EMD had no FT to spare for wartime demonstration purposes, and few railroads had locomotives they would willingly loan to another. The O&W therefore had to rely on its own analysis of data collected by EMD and other railroads.

Through this analysis, O&W officials calculated that the road would save more than $1 million per year in costs associated with steam operation (including 266,000 helper- and 120,000 light-engine-miles and $57,000 in fuel handling and car-hire costs). Armed with these impressive figures, the O&W trustee received authority from the court on July 3, 1944, to place an order for 37 diesel-electric locomotives at a cost $6.7 million.

The 37-diesel count had been determined by a committee of O&W operating men and EMD people. They selected a "base" day which represented the peak traffic conditions and locomotive needs. The day chosen was Oct. 26, 1943. The locomotive needs were to be met by two models, FT's and NW2's. The FT fleet was to be comprised of four A-B-B-A, one A-B-A and eight A-B sets and eight single A units. The 16 NW2's were divided with ten assigned to road switching and six to yard service. Grand total: 59 individual units with a total of 74,050 h.p. The purchase order had a clause permitting the count to be modified, and in fact it would be—several times.

Not surprising, the O&W was, during these planning stages, still working with a steam-locomotive-assignment mentality. It would be fascinating to have been party to the discussions between EMD representatives (the "party of the future") and the O&W people (the "party of the past") to see how they worked out the plan of change. For example, there is scant photographic evidence that any of the Class I railroads owning FT's operated them as single units in regular practice as the O&W planned to do. The idea of operating them in fixed sets of single and double units was scrapped when it became evident that the plan was too expensive, but we will later find the O&W purchasing and equipping individual F3A's for road switching.

After Lyford's resignation in December 1944, the new co-trustees, Raymond L. Gebhardt and Ferdinand J. Sieghardt, soon told the court that complete dieselization was neither feasible nor advisable at the time and that it would be best to limit diesel purchases to nine sets of FT's, costing $2.2 million (approximately $250,000 per unit). Of this amount, nearly $1.7 million was to be raised by sale of an entire issue of Equipment Trust Certificates, called the "New York, Ontario & Western Equipment Trust of 1945," to the Reconstruction Finance Corporation. Central Hanover Bank & Trust Company of New York was designated as trustee of the equipment trust and would hold title to the locomotives and lease them to the railroad. The trust was to mature on May 1, 1955; the date of the formal contracting with EMD for the FT's appears to have been April 14, 1945.

An additional loan source for the railroad's dieselization was the Standard Oil Development Company, which was looking for a "test lab" where advanced diesel fuels and lubricants could be developed. SOD agreed to finance one A-B set—the 601—for testing purposes.

A certain amount of the financing, of course, had to come from the O&W itself. In the spring of 1945, the railroad sold 34 steel passenger cars (which it had earlier leased to Atlantic Coast Line and Seaboard Air Line) for $255,000 and 23 wooden coaches for $50,600. Also sold in that period were 30 steam locomotives, 50 freight cars and 12,780 tons of rail and track fastenings rendered surplus through the single-tracking of much of the Mayfield-Cornwall line. Together these sales yielded $430,000, which was applied to the purchase of the diesels and related costs of dieselization.

But dieselization meant more than just buying locomotives. Fuel and lube-oil tanks, piping and associated pumps would be necessary at both Middletown and Mayfield—at a cost of $12,720. Smaller fueling stations already existed for the 44-tonners, but operations called for the road diesels to be fueled at Middletown or Mayfield. As built, the Middletown tanks held 26,000 gallons of fuel and the Mayfield tanks 27,000 gallons, but shortly afterward each facility was expanded to hold 76,000 gallons. (With the 1948 acquisition of 27 more units, Middletown received two additional 25,000-gallon tanks, and a 100,000-gallon tank was installed at Mayfield.) In addition, O&W had to purchase a stock of repair parts from EMD—to be primarily dispensed from Middletown—for nearly $106,000.

Major changes had to be made to the Middletown shop facilities and, to a lesser extent, the facilities at Mayfield and other terminals. Track pits, elevated servicing platforms, parts storage racks and parts cleaning and reconditioning rooms had to be constructed in the erecting shop. Wheel, traction motor and general diesel-truck servicing required a Whiting side-release

While riding an excursion that was handled as part of a regular passenger train, Hal Carstens leaned from his coach to catch a meet at a forgotten location. Centralized Traffic Control (CTC), seen in action here, allowed the O&W to remove one of its two main tracks between Cadosia and Middletown with the exception of strategically located passing sections.—HAL CARSTENS.

drop table that permitted the complete exchange of a locomotive truck in a matter of hours. Electrical and mechanical testing equipment had to be purchased, with some items being constructed by shop forces. Building alterations required by the new motive power including the relocation of piping, electrical lines and other utilities brought the total cost for this part of the dieselization program to over $100,000. Not all of this work was done prior to the arrival of the FT's; in fact, much of it was not finished until the arrival of the F3's and NW2's in 1948.

EMD had O&W's FT's finished and ready for delivery before the financing was completed. Rather than delay the employment of the locomotives, the railroad leased the units from EMD under a short-term contact at the rate of $20 per day per A-B set until June 30, 1945. By that time the railroad was using the units under the terms of the equipment trust.

The diesels arrived on the O&W in late spring 1945. O&W men were sent to LaGrange and rode units 801-804 and 601 east, under their own power, over the Erie to Maybrook, N.Y., where they were interchanged to the O&W. The same delivery plan was used for locomotives 805-808 which arrived a little later. Since the units were actually working on freight trains for the greater part of the trip, the only shipping charges were some $50 per set for transfer from LaGrange to the Erie at Hammond, Ind.

The O&W people got valuable on-the-job training by having experienced Erie crews and EMD field instructors in the cab with them. There was also the advantage of getting the units delivered quicker than if they had been towed dead in a train and of having them broken-in under the supervision of qualified personnel. While moving east along the Erie, it was discovered that one set of units had metal turnings left in a gearbox. It went into Erie's shop at Marion, Ohio, for repairs and was back on the road within 24 hours.

An hour after leaving Maybrook, the new diesels arrived in Middletown where employees and townspeople came out to view and tour the O&W's colorful saviors. Within a few days, shop forces added a number of details that made the units unique to O&W. Coat hooks, lockers, tools, stenciled instructions and additional warnings were placed inside the units. Several external features were applied over a longer period of time, including the reflectorized number plates attached to the nose door just below the red O&W emblem and, on A-units, an electrical receptacle behind the pilot to supply power for snowplow headlights.

In addition, three grab irons were placed on tops of each nose to provide a hand- or foothold when cleaning windshields. Rerailing frogs were hung under each side at the rear of the B unit, and toward the rear of the B-unit roof, just behind the rear set of radiator fans, was a rectangular device that covered a hole in the roof. This boxy device had a telescoping section that could be slid forward to cover approximately one-third of the rear radiator fan and direct the captured heated air back into the rear of the B unit. So far as can be determined, the purpose of this deflected air was to keep the toilet water from freezing in cold weather. The first application of this device is believed to have been to the 601 in February 1946. The Lackawanna had similar devices on its FTB units and because its locomotives were in service earlier, it's possible that the O&W copied Lackawanna's idea.

Another O&W-inspired alteration was the two-position (versus the factory-delivered single-position) sanding valve. In the forward position, only the forward sander for the front truck operated; the rear position opened all truck sanders. Apparently this arrangement worked best on units equipped with 65:12 gearing due to certain idiosyncrasies of this gear ratio. Originally, this gearing limited the FT's to a top speed of 45 mph, but in September 1946 the railroad contacted EMD about raising the top speed to 50. EMD advised that the units were already perfectly capable of 50 mph, but at a slight reduction of horsepower. At about the same time, easi-

Crewman look back for a signal on the inside of the curve between the station and the yard in Middletown. This is the pre-radio age in railroading, so fusees, lanterns and hand signals—often relayed over the length of a 100-car train—were the means of communication. It's a good bet that the orange hopper car behind the units belongs to the Waddell Coal Co. of Winton, Pa.—MARV COHEN.

er-to-read transition meter dials were installed in the locomotive cabs, showing the short-time overload period calibrated in miles rather than minutes. (Diesel-locomotive traction motors may be put under electrical overload for short periods to overcome certain operational problems—starting a train on a grade for example—but should an engineer exceed the time limit, the traction motors might burn out.)

Nominally, each A-B set weighed approximately 230 tons and had a tractive effort of 114,500 pounds. These figures did not include the weight of extra equipment, fuel and whatever ballasting the railroad later added.

The O&W's choice of a paint scheme and colors resulted in a design that was quite individualistic, although the scheme per se was designed by EMD and not O&W people. EMD's Styling Section, which in those days provided railroads with suggested paint schemes, often used common elements—for example, "sweep" stripes—which could be found on various roads' schemes. In the case of O&W's FT livery, the upper thin stripe with the arrow was right out of EMD's design book, but the other elements—although harboring some EMD-esque characteristics—were untried elsewhere, and the overall appearance of the scheme was unique.

Correspondence between O&W officials and EMD's New York sales people indicated that the road originally had planned to apply its initials to the sides of the units, but in the end, only red O&W heralds on the nose and the sides identified the company's diesels. There were no other initials or company name—a practice few other mainline carriers followed (PRR's late 1960's "keystone phase" comes to mind). Although O&W's scheme was not intricate, glamorous or regal in the sense of, say, Santa Fe's warbonnet or Baltimore & Ohio's blue and gray, it was graceful, in simple taste and provided visibility contrast.

There was also ample discussion among top operating men regarding the numbering of the new diesels. One proposal featured an alpha-numeric system that would have resulted in two different designations per unit. The amount of discussion and complexity involved with determining a numbering system was staggering but somewhat understandable in view of potential train-identification problems and pay claims from labor unions. This latter point was especially sensitive for many railroads in that enginemen might claim extra pay for operation of two, three or more units. Using a single number with suffix

The 803 bursts into daylight exiting the south portal of Bloomingburg Tunnel. The dripping blackness of the bore always posed a threat of fallen rock and an unplanned stop in the tunnel. Such a stop could result in asphyxiation of crew members, and the diesels themselves might even shut down if they could not get an adequate supply of air. The threat was greater with steam locomotives since gases were produced in larger quantities, and many men were indeed overcome through the years.—MARV COHEN.

tion procedures had to be followed to see that critical oil and fuel pressures and engine temperatures were normal. One notice said that firemen were expected to walk through the engine rooms every 15 minutes.

The high-voltage warning signs throughout engine rooms made some railroaders absolutely paranoid. Until they found they were not going to be electrocuted if they touched any metal surface, some men refused to walk through to the toilet in the B unit and instead stopped the train and got off to answer a call of nature.

ACCORDING TO the *Scranton Tribune*, the 801 was the first of five locomotives to arrive on the railroad, and it made its first revenue run on May 16, 1945. It had officially entered service the previous day with General Road Foreman Guy S. Bennett at the throttle. Trustee Gebhardt was also in the cab as was Col. Noten D. Ballantine, the special consultant influential in the railroad's dieselization.

For the first revenue run, the 801 led a four-unit consist that hauled a 100-car train of tank cars on a six-hour run (origin not noted). Oscar O. Bennett, brother of the road foreman, was the engineer.

(ABOVE) The distinctive windshield of an F-unit frames a southward view of the upper end of Middletown Yard where a lone NW2 readies a string of cars for pickup. The many empty tracks bode ill of the road's future.—JIM SHAUGHNESSY. (RIGHT) Engineer Elwood Worden pulls the horn rope in the cab of an FT. The clearance form and train order authorizing this trip are visible on the clipboard between the transition/dynamic brake lever on the right and the unit selector switch at left.—GUY TWADDELL PHOTO, JOE BOX COLLECTION.

letters and/or the use of drawbars in place of couplers between units allowed railroads to claim that the crew was handling one locomotive regardless of how many units it was composed.

As virtually all railroads did when they got their first diesels, the O&W operated them like steam engines. They were pampered and spent a good deal of time in engine terminals with frequent inspections and service time that exceeded EMD requirements. As time went on, railroads began to realize that the new locomotives were not all that delicate. Nonetheless, there were a host of small details that enginemen had to understand and respect if the locomotives were to perform properly and provide all the cost-saving advantages expected of them.

Many habits and procedures relating to the operation of steam locomotives that had been acquired through years of conditioning had to be set aside when enginemen were called for a diesel-powered train. Throttles had to be notched down when crossing other railroads at grade lest wheel slip would gouge the rails and cause arcing between traction motor brushes and commutator. All engineroom doors had to be kept closed so that only filtered air would enter the prime mover and traction motor blowers. Many inspec-

Realizing that he would have a clean new diesel, he did not wear his usual garb of denim shirt, coveralls and gloves. To his chagrin, however, he did not make the return run on the 801 but instead drew one of the big, slow and dirty X-class 2-10-2 "Bull Moose" types. His sport clothes did not fare too well and without a heavy collar and bandanna, he complained of getting lots of cinders down his neck.

Between early November and Christmas 1945, EMD training car 100 visited Mayfield, Cadosia, Norwich and Middletown. Classes were provided for all employees who would work with the new locomotives in either operational or maintenance roles. This was in addition to the instruction given to supervisory people sent earlier to EMD's school at LaGrange.

FT 601 and the Standard Oil Development Tests

Dieselized American railroads were going to provide a much larger market for oil company products than they had for steam power. Yet much had to be learned about diesel road locomotives and the conditions in which they operated. With the removal of war-imposed restrictions and priorities, the need for more-extensive testing was both necessary and possible. Standard Oil Development Company (SOD), a research and development affiliate of the Standard Oil Company (Esso), had the choice of buying its own test locomotive and conducting the research in its own labs or of getting the cooperation of a nearby railroad and experiencing "real world" conditions. SOD chose the latter course.

SOD had several reasons for choosing the O&W as the field lab. The railroad was already an Esso customer, and the Middletown shop location was reasonably close to SOD's metropolitan New York office to permit establishment of an operations base as well as frequent in-person communication with administrative and mechanical officers. The O&W was purchasing EMD road units exclusively, and EMD represented the greatest percentage of diesels in service. The rugged terrain over which the O&W operated offered high load factors—a prerequisite in testing crankcase lubricants. And, since the O&W was a relatively small railroad in both area of service and size of staff, it was easier to exercise control over the operation of the test units.

The road's FT's were equipped with a 65:12 gear ratio which was the lowest available from EMD and certainly in line with the road's physical profile. This ratio meant the units could be subjected to the most severe service conditions since they could be operated as slowly as 11 mph at full throttle with a tonnage train. Finally, by advancing the railroad the purchase price of the locomotive, SOD could have its "own" diesel for testing on a property that actually appreciated the help. The railroad got $249,341 in financing from SOD for FT set 601, and consequently SOD had a large say in how and where it was to be used. The loan was to be repaid in three installments at no interest. (At least one-third of the loan was repaid.)

An agreement between SOD and the O&W, dated April 23, 1945, covered the financial transaction, allowed for supervised inspections and overhauls, permitted SOD to install a number of measuring instruments in the units and allowed their personnel to ride the locomotive whenever necessary. By this agreement, the locomotive was restricted to hauling freight between Maybrook and Mayfield Yard at Scranton.

SOD's test people got to work on May 21, 1945, when the 601 arrived in Middletown. Thermocouples and gauges were installed in the units to monitor lube oil, cooling water and exhaust temperatures and to record critical pressures. The railroad was not yet fully equipped to maintain and service the new diesels, and this was vividly illustrated when the 601 came in from the Erie. The lube oil had to be immediately changed for a test oil charge, and SOD men had to hastily organize a bucket brigade to refill the crankcase with some 200 gallons of new oil.

The total program consisted of sets of individual tests. Before each test, the 601 would enter the shop to receive new cylinder liners, pistons, rings and other parts. Prior to installation, these parts were carefully measured and weighed. After removing all traces of previous lube oil, a new charge was pumped into the crankcase. The oil was carefully checked numerous times during the ensuing test period. After a predetermined period of time had passed, the units would again be shopped and all parts would again be quantitatively evaluated and the differences recorded. All the work had to be done in an exact and precise manner if the results were to present a true picture. For this reason, the 601 was not to move without SOD knowledge. On at least one occasion, however, this did happen, and several O&W people were called on the carpet. This must have been a rare occurrence since SOD personnel said the cooperation of O&W people was excellent.

Since SOD used only new parts at the start of each test and since the life expectancy of the parts was well in excess of test duration, the railroad built up a nice supply of liners, pistons and other power-assembly components at modest cost. Originally the test program was to last three years, but a clause in the contract allowed SOD an option to extend the test period from year to year beyond the original May 1, 1948, contract termination date with SOD paying the railroad $25,000 per year for such cooperation. It is believed that extensions did in fact take place. Following the 601 lube oil tests, experimental diesel fuel evaluations involving all road units were conducted until 1951. The O&W got some free publicity when Esso ran ads, mentioning the railroad, in the trade press.

The lube-oil tests were significant in that advanced diesel oil technology was evaluated for the first time—so it was claimed—in a full-scale operation under closely controlled conditions.

Ray Brown stood on Erie's Graham Line bridge about a mile north of Campbell Hall to photograph FT sets 804 and 808 rolling north with 93 cars on March 24, 1946. This former-Erie bridge still crosses the O&W right-of-way and is still called "O&W bridge" by Conrail and Metro-North crews.—RAY W. BROWN.

Four FT sets meet at Crawford Junction, N.Y., juncture with Erie's Pine Bush Branch. This was also the end of double track that began at East Main Street in Middletown. Erie used the O&W from Middletown to Crawford Junction.—BOTH PHOTOS, MARV COHEN.

Straight mineral oils proved to be inadequate in protecting moving parts in the EMD engines that were developing ever higher horsepower. Compounded lubricants incorporating the use of detergents, anti-oxidants and other additives were required to adequately cope with the higher demands being placed upon diesel motive power.

At the time of the 601 program, O&W was the only road employed by SOD. Due to the increasingly higher demands made by larger and more-powerful diesels, subsequent tests became necessary, and the Nashville, Chattanooga & St. Louis, Lehigh Valley, Lackawanna, New Haven, Norfolk & Western, Baltimore & Ohio, Penn Central and Southern Pacific all served at one time or another as SOD's cooperating roads up to 1971.

Clem Bovio, one of the SOD men involved with the 601, relates two instances which still stood out in his memory some 25 years after their occurrence. He recalled that 601's first northbound trip was uneventful until the locomotive and its train approached Carbondale, near Scranton. As the new diesel rolled down the valley, the crew was greeted with .22-caliber rifle fire. It seems the arrival of an oil-fueled diesel locomotive was not exactly good news to the local anthracite coal industry and the men who depended upon it for a living. (This story has been substantiated by an inspection report at Middletown that listed bullet holes in the sides of FT's.) Bovio also said that a special "Purple Heart Award" was created by the EMD operating instructors and SOD men and presented to their colleagues who survived the gun fire and had successfully negotiated the high "swaying trestles" of the O&W.

Numbering a Diesel Roster

THE INTRODUCTION OF MULTIPLE-UNIT DIESELS gave rise to serious concerns regarding pay for engine crews. Two or more steam locomotives on the point of a train meant pay for each locomotive's crew and that was that. How would the unions react to two or more units—considered to be a single locomotive—under the control of one crew in the first unit? Although locomotive crews had been assigned to multiple-unit electric locomotives on, for example, the New Haven and New York Central for many years and were not receiving additional pay, it seemed to be a different issue with internal-combustion locomotives. One of the diesel's greatest appeals to management was that it could cut down the costs of engine crews as well as maintenance labor. If the enginemens' unions forced the railroads to pay locomotive crews on the number of units or to employ additional men, one of the diesels' big advantages would be lost.

The drawbar coupling of the FT eased some of those concerns since the railroads felt they had a strong case in pointing out that the B unit could not operate independently. One idea, used successfully by many railroads, was to assign a single number to a locomotive regardless of the number of units in its makeup.

Before the FT's arrived, the O&W pondered the numbering arrangement at some length. At first the railroad planned to have each unit identified by two letters. Each of the nine FT A units would carry the letter A followed by a second letter beginning with A and running through to I. Thus the A units would be identified as AA to AI while the nine B units would be lettered BA to BI. It does not appear that the letters would be hyphenated nor would they be used for operational identification. Rather, the locomotive sets assembled from these units would be identified by numbers. Since O&W's steam roster ended at 460 (the last Y-2-class 4-8-2 of 1929), it was logical for the road to number the diesels in the 500's. This they did but not in the manner expected. The railroad decided that single-unit road diesels would be in the 500 series, two-unit locomotives would be 600's, three units would be 700's and four units would be 800's. How the road planned to operate single-unit or three-unit FT sets when they were semi-permanently coupled in AB sets remains a mystery.

To carry out this cumbersome numbering scheme, each unit was to carry an adequate supply of loose numerals that could be easily inserted into number-board slots; this constant numbering and renumbering would probably have been the responsibility of the terminal hostler or the fireman before a run began. In theory, FT A unit "AB" might have operated as a single unit, numbered 501, on one day, as the lead of two-unit locomotive 601 the next day, and the 701 on an A-B-B combination the third day. The question arises then: Who would assign these numbers so that another A unit leading a three-unit set would not also be designated 701 at the same time? Clearly, this could have led to serious operational problems and its possible the Interstate Commerce Commission vetoed this scheme as one old-timer reported.

It seems strange that the experiences and practices of more than 20 other railroads that employed FT's were not simply followed right from the start. A very successful and simple scheme employed by many lines was to assign one number to a two-, three- or four-unit locomotive and use a suffix letter or digit to identify the individual units. By the time the FT's arrived from EMD, this simple scheme was wisely adopted but part of the original idea—that of locomotive numbering based upon number of units—was carried through to a degree. Three F3 A units delivered in 1948 were initially assigned to road-switching tasks and were expected to work as single-unit locomotives; they were numbered in the 500's. A single FT set, the 601, was carried on the books as a two-unit locomotive even though it frequently operated with other units. There were no "fixed" three-unit locomotives, so the 700 series remained vacant of any diesels. (Knowledgeable O&W historians will recall that a D&H Camelback 2-8-0 was purchased in 1947 to handle a temporary increase in business. It was numbered 701 and was in active service for less than a year).

The eight FT sets were considered to be configured into four 5400-h.p. A-B-B-A locomotives and were given 800-series numbers. The other four F3's purchased in 1948, two A's and two B's, were also considered to be a single, four-unit locomotive and became the 821 and 822. The NW2's simply followed the precedent set by the 44-tonners in 1941; they went into the 100 series as single-unit switchers—R.M.

Almost half of the railroad's FT fleet is tied up at Mayfield Yard in this photograph taken by O&W conductor Guy Twaddell. Mayfield was built as a coal marshalling yard, and it was actually at some distance from through traffic connections which were geographically south. A-B sets of FT's and F3's frequently shuttled through-line cars between those connections and Mayfield. NW2's, of course, were assigned to yard itself but also handled transfers of through-line cars.—GUY TWADDELL.

The Flying Diesel Corps

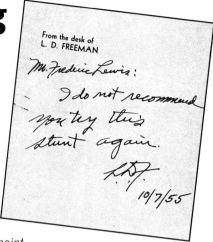

ON THE DARK, RAINY NIGHT of Sept. 27, 1955, train ON-2 rumbled into Hamilton, N.Y., as it had done so many times before. Engineer Les Vidler had FT 803 on a 50-car train that night and was making about 34 mph when he—or someone else in the cab— noticed that a mainline facing-point switch was set for a siding leading up to Leland's coal trestle. The engineer quickly applied the brakes, but the momentum was enough to push the train up the siding, through the coal-shed doors and the barnlike structure and out the opposite end. After the noise ended and debris settled, it was found that the 213-ton locomotive had "flown" 150 feet beyond the end of the coal trestle after taking off from an elevation of 15 feet. The drawbar between the A and B units snapped, and four cars had followed the air-borne FT's. A fifth car hung off the end of the trestle. Two men in the 803's cab, Road Foreman of Engines Fred Lewis and fireman Oliver Wrench, were seriously injured.

Several theories were advanced as to who threw the switch, but, so far as is known, a state police investigation did not result in any arrests. At a dinner honoring the crewmen for their skill, courage and devotion to duty, Trustee Lewis D. Freeman said that the men had been air borne for about six or seven seconds. Each crewman received a plaque and a cast model presentation F-unit courtesy of EMD. Road Foreman Lewis also got a special note advising him ". . . not to try this stunt again." The 803 returned to service following repairs at Middletown.

One of the cars involved in the wreck was loaded with chocolate bars from the Nestle plant in Fulton. Local people soon cleaned it out, and little if any candy was sold in Hamilton for some time!—R.M.

O&W Diesel Utilization and Assignment

Long before the FT's arrived, Middletown's motive-power and operating departments put a great deal of planning into how the new diesels could be most efficiently deployed. Plans were drawn up and frequently revised as the number of units ordered was changed. By February 1945, the following arrangements had been decided upon: Two four-unit, 5400-h.p. sets were to be assigned to the Mayfield-Maybrook through freights, roughly a 270-mile round trip. A third four-unit set would handle a 210-mile round trip with through freight between Mayfield and Norwich, and a two-unit 2700-h.p. set was to be assigned to combined passenger and milk trains 1-9 and 2-10 between Weehawken and Cadosia, a round trip of 320 miles. The remaining two 2700-h.p. locomotives were not given specific assignments but represented one protection set and one set going through the regular maintenance cycle.

When the road diesels arrived, a modified plan was put into effect. The competitively sensitive southbound time freights NE-2, NE-4 and NE-6 and their northbound counterparts BC-l, BC-3 and an Extra North operating between the Wyoming Valley and Maybrook, were assigned two four-unit FT sets. (In reality, it appears there was insufficient diesel power to cover these runs, and ten 4-8-2's were still in service to fill in where needed, including frequent turns on the time freights.) The proposed FT passenger assignment was eliminated, and a diesel protection locomotive was judged too expensive a luxury. The milk and passenger runs were therefore usually assigned steam power, and a 4-8-2 covered the protection requirements. These changes provided another 5400-h.p. set for revenue-producing freight tonnage.

The through runs frequently included making direct connections with either or both the DL&W at Cayuga Junction (a 28-mile round trip out of Mayfield) and the LV at Coxton Yard (a 48-mile round trip from Mayfield), which required considerable additional time. A third set of four units eased the tight schedules for these important runs. An inspection of dispatchers' train sheets from the 1950's indicated that O&W often was running the road power through to these connections, but there was no evidence to indicate that the practice was reciprocal; i.e., that DL&W or LV crews and power came into Mayfield. (LV would occasionally provide a pusher crew between Coxton and Sibley Junction if an O&W train was returning to Mayfield by that route. Coxton to Cayuga Junction via DL&W's Bloomsburg Branch and Hampton Yard was the preferred route account of easier grades.)

Until 1948, when they were replaced by the NW2's, smaller steam locomotives were often used between Mayfield Yard and the connections down the valley. If a return train was not ready, these crews and locomotives sometimes tied up at Coxton and came back "on their rest" or when a return through connection came in off the LV or DL&W. When the connection transfers arrived back at Mayfield, local cars from O&W origins and cars from the D&H and Jersey Central were added to the through cars and the train was dispatched for Maybrook. The practice of using steam or NW2's to run the connections gave the FT's more time at Mayfield for servicing. The three Maybrook-Mayfield round trips were later reduced to two with extra trains operated as needed.

Another pair of symbol freights operated between Mayfield Yard and Utica. SU-1 and US-2 were assigned FT's between Mayfield and Norwich while W-class 2-8-0's (later NW2's) provided power between Norwich and Utica. Although the Utica Branch could handle FT's, they usually did not wander from the main line.

The assignment of an A-B set to milk trains 1

and 10 between Weehawken and Cadosia may have occurred briefly, but there is little evidence that this was a regular practice. But FT's certainly did see passenger service during the busy summer season when passenger schedules were increased to accommodate Catskill-bound tourists. Steam power continued in passenger service until the F3's arrived in 1948.

FT's may have worked the northern end of the WA-1 and AW-2 runs, a semi-local through freight operating between Weehawken and Oswego and combined with SU-1 and US-2 between Cadosia and Norwich. The train's final 100 miles between Norwich and Oswego were diesel-powered only if the more-important Mayfield-Maybrook trains had been covered first. Later, WA-1 and AW-2 were replaced by ON-1 and NO-2 between Norwich and Oswego. This train pair operated as a "two-sided turn" six days per week with an FT set. This meant one train left Norwich and one left Oswego daily (except Sunday), so a crew made a round trip in two days and provided six-day service in both directions. (A "one-sided" job would provide alternate -direction, six-day service. The Monticello and Port Jervis branches had such service, but these branches did not see FT's.)

MAKING CONNECTIONS, both with foreign lines and within the O&W's own network of operations, called for careful planning and coordination, but there were frequent delays and occasional mechanical problems that kept diesels from meeting scheduled runs. Dispatchers' diaries often reported the substitution of steam power if a connection was late or if a diesel set could not make a terminal in time for a return run. If NE-4 was going to be late getting into

Maybrook and its FT set was marked to bring BC-1 out, a Y-class 4-8-2 would be dispatched from Middletown to substitute. Diesels on US-2, handling livestock traffic from the NYC at Utica, would probably not wait at Norwich for a late AW-2. AW-2's W-class steamer might instead go through to Cadosia, or the Norwich protection locomotive might be used to take the train south.

A little arithmetic indicates that the FT's were covering approximately 1,026 miles-per-day which averages out to 146 miles per 2700-h.p. set, but the O&W claimed an average of 177 miles-per-day—which is what EMD had projected in its 1944 report. For comparison, neighboring Reading Railroad was reporting approximately 200 miles-per-day for its FT's while Great Northern was logging more than 300 miles-per-day. These are very low figures compared to what diesels cover on a daily basis today, but of course many factors have changed since then.

For over a dozen years, O&W's nine FT's rolled through the mountains of New York and Pennsylvania, along the East Branch and the Beaverkill rivers, over NYC's West Shore Route and through the flat country north of Oneida. At least one set was leased to the D&H to reduce steam mileage when a soft-coal strike put a pinch on the locomotive fuel supply. In addition, O&W FT's detoured over neighboring roads a number of times when derailments or acts of nature put parts of the railroad out of service, and they survived numerous mishaps which resulted in scraped paint, dented metal and patchwork. It does not appear that the locomotives were ever repainted, but significant amounts of touch-up work are evident in several photographs.

Despite the road's poor economic condition, the units were never allowed to become filthy,

An unusual meet on the Carbondale trestle finds southbound FT's leading a freight past an F3 toting a caboose and combine—in reality a fan trip sponsored by the Joint Railfan Trip Committee, a consortium of New York Metropolitan area clubs that organized trips for its members. The date is June 19, 1948.—JOHN PICKETT.

(RIGHT) On March 23, 1957, FT 806 was dispatched northward from Cadosia with a single boxcar and caboose. Near Maywood, the train rolls through an early spring landscape. Since the railroad is on an 800-foot descent from Northfield Tunnel, the locomotive is under no strain.

(ABOVE) We're north of Sidney, and now the FT is working, roaring up the grade toward Oxford and Summit with a train of cars it picked up from the D&H at Sidney. (RIGHT) The 806 crosses the Chenango River and enters Norwich yard just a few days before the court-ordered termination of operations.—THREE PHOTOS, JOHN D. HAHN JR.

and many employees maintained that diligent, first-class mechanical attention was reflected by the locomotives' external appearances. This was confirmed by a letter from Superintendent Fred Hawk which stated that the O&W's diesels were shopped less frequently for employees' carelessness or negligence than those of many other roads. In July 1953, Mr. William F. Mathieson, chief accounting officer for the railroad, was questioned on the quality of that care during a hearing at which the RFC was attempting

to repossess the diesels:

Q. Now, both as to the 1945 and 1947 equipment, how has it been maintained?

A. Ever since we have acquired these locomotives, we have been very careful to keep these locomotives in perfect running condition. We have taken extraordinary care of them. We have been, if I might say, the envy of many of the other railroads [in terms of] the way our locomotives are performing and the condition we keep them in. All the railroads with whom we do business come over to our shop and credit us for the condition of our engines and our diesel shops.

Q. What about the manufacturer?

A. The men from the manufacturer come down from time to time and they are also very pleased and gratified with the condition of the engines.

Q. You mean the inspecting force of the General Motors Corporation, the Electro Motive Division of the General Motors Corporation?

A. That is correct.

An additional confirmation of the excellent maintenance that O&W gave its diesels came from the Northern Pacific, which purchased NW2 No. 115 in 1957. NP's mechanical department stated, "Our inspection of this locomotive showed . . . the general condition of the diesel engine being very good."

With the GE 44-tonners in place and the FT's well established within the O&W family, the Phase II story of O&W's dieselization process comes to an end. Phase III of the diesel program would make life easier for motive-power dispatchers. Beginning in the summer of 1948, they would have three times the number of diesels to work with.

(ABOVE) Still identifiable by the nose wrinkles resulting from a grade-crossing accident while on the O&W, former 807 A&B is now B&O 4413 and 5413 sitting at Benwood Junction, W.Va., on April 6, 1958. Additional grab irons have been added to the roof and ladder rests on the nose for access to the windshields.—JAY POTTER COLLECTION.
(BELOW) US-2 crosses Cadosia Creek with a train that originated at Canal Yard in Utica around the nucleus of an NYC delivery. The train was reclassified at Cadosia with the addition or removal of Southern Division cars. The power on this train—and its counterpart, SU-1—usually ran through between Norwich and Mayfield.—HAL CARSTENS.

5/The EMD NW2's

The O&W's successful experience with the 44-tonners during World War II proved the advantages of dieselized switching operations. This, coupled with the reliability, savings and overall performance of the FT road diesels, pointed toward dieselization of all switching operations. Electro-Motive's diesel switchers had been employed longer than its diesel road freight units, and their advantages over steam operation had been documented for fifteen years or more. With O&W's decision to undertake the third and final phase of dieselization, EMD was again chosen as the manufacturer. Neither the railroad nor EMD lost sight of the original plan and agreement to completely dieselize operations with Electro-Motive power.

The War Production Board edict directing EMD to suspend switcher production between April 1943 and January 1945 would have adversely affected O&W's dieselization program if the road had been able to implement it in its entirety at the time. However, war priorities and

O&W's cash position had delayed the program. Meanwhile, EMD continued to improve its locomotive line including the temporarily suspended switchers, as evidenced by the fact that it referred to its pre-war switchers as "earlier locomotives" and postwar production as "later locomotives," although the same model designations continued to be used.

EMC's first switchers were built in 1935 for the DL&W and used Winton engines and electrical components furnished by General Electric who also did the assembly at one of its facilities. The two units, powered by 600-h.p. engines, established the characteristic EMC—and later EMD—switcher configuration. Although the pioneering pair bore similarities to earlier American Locomotive Company and Baldwin Locomotive Works diesel switchers, they did not appear to have as high a center of gravity as did the Alco and Baldwin units of the period. The roofs of the engine hood were flat and the general boxy appearance of the units was broken only by

(LEFT AND BELOW) Winter snows dust the grounds of the EMD plant near Chicago as NW2 113 poses for the EMD photographer in 1948. It seems strange that, under its financial circumstances, O&W would outlay additional money in having manufactured logos for the noses of the NW2's. The NW2 was EMD's best-selling switcher, and since it no longer produces such designs, that's a record that should last. The styling was highly functional. One can find few, if any, lines that did not have utilitarian purpose. Good visibility, ease of maintenance, cost of manufacture and economy of operation stood above all else. Yet there is an obvious and satisfactory reminder of the steam heritage in the high headlight, curved cab roof, long walkway and handrail and the high-mounted bell. All strike a chord in "the remembrance of things past."—BOTH PHOTOS, COURTESY EMD.

(FACING PAGE) The NW2's were part of O&W's 1947 diesel order, which included the F3's. Here at Middletown, NW2 127 idles as a lengthy passenger train behind F3 502 undergoes an inspection before leaving for Weehawken. The 127 may be "on the spot"(a railroader's expression for taking a break), or it is assigned to a job that goes to work at this location.—DON WALLWORTH.

arched cab roofs and a few curved corners. The large behind-the-cab battery box made its appearance on these first switchers.

EMC's third switcher produced 900 h.p. and was assembled by Bethlehem Steel using Westinghouse electrical gear and control equipment. Numbered 518 and first used as a demonstrator, it differed significantly in appearance from the first two units in that it bore a crude resemblance to a road-switcher. It is possible that EMC produced a few other models that were assembled in subcontractors' shops. In any event, these early designs were evaluated to determine which models were to be produced at LaGrange when that new facility opened.

By May 1936 the plant had been completed and EMC turned out its first "home-built" switcher, which was constructed for the Santa Fe and designated model SC—the "S" standing for 600 h.p. and the "C" for cast frame. (Welded locomotive components, especially frames, were suspect by many railroad mechanical officers.

Until time had proven them sound, many railroads preferred the more-expensive cast frames. Eventually, the cast-frame option was dropped). In this unit, EMC cleaned up the design it had introduced in the two Lackawanna units of 1935. The cab was made roomier and wider, and deeper windows were provided for almost 360-degree visibility. Additionally, the SC set the 44-foot 6-inch length that was to be standard for EMD switchers for more than two decades.

In addition to the 518, a number of other models in the 900-h.p. range were produced in this period as well. All bore the same style carbody of the 600-h.p. switcher but were designated NC or NW models. As was noted in the FT chapter, EMC during this period was tooling up to meet its own subassembly and electrical equipment requirements. Sometime in 1939, the task was essentially completed and EMC no longer needed to rely on subcontractors for electrical gear. That was also the year that the 600-h.p. SW1 and 1000-h.p. NW2 were introduced.

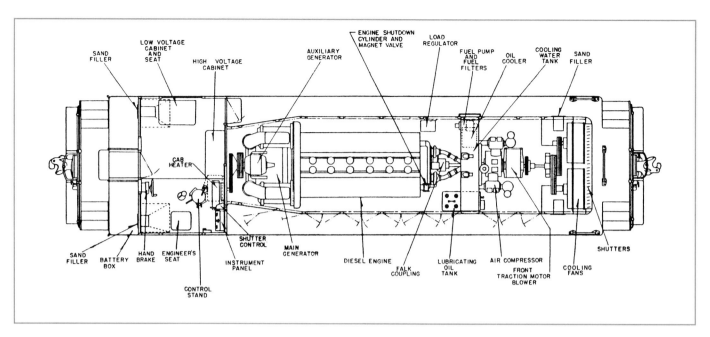

When O&W finally ordered big switchers in 1947, EMD was still offering the SW1 and NW2. Since their introduction in 1939, they had far out-sold the combined production of other builders' comparable switchers. The two models were produced concurrently until late 1949 when the NW2 was superseded by a higher-horsepower unit.

In the model designations SW1 and NW2, the "W" signified welded frame. The "S" meant 600 h.p. and the "N" meant 900 h.p.—the ratings of earlier models; illogically, the N had been carried into the designation of the 1000-h.p. units.

To save on production costs, both the SW1 and the NW2 used the same frame. This resulted in noticeably longer platforms on the front and rear of the SW1 since it used a shorter engine hood. Early SW1's and NW2's had the short, stubby exhaust stacks of the FT, but these were later changed to the tall, conical stacks that are typical of EMD switchers to this day. It is likely that the short stacks did not lift the ex-

(LEFT) With a man in every door, this photo resembles a publicity shot, but it does show the accessibility that EMD designed into the NW2's. Latching doors and hatches permitted easy access to the engine compartment. The scene also calls to mind the comment of a veteran roundhouse foreman who made an interesting comparison between steam and diesel: He said a problem on a steam engine could be found in five minutes and took a day to repair; on a diesel it took a day to find and five minutes to repair. (BELOW) Modifications are being made to the Middletown erecting shop so that it will be better able to accommodate diesel locomotives. An additional high-level platform is underway in the foreground.—BOTH PHOTOS, O&W SOCIETY COLLECTION.

(BELOW) "Bundled-up," so to speak, the 114, working Middletown yard, has a canvas cover over half the radiator air intake grille on the nose to help maintain proper engine operating temperature. Excessive cool air could be as problematic as not enough.—COURTESY OF RAILROAD AVENUE ENTERPRISES.

Number 131, the last unit in the NW2 order, idles at Cadosia on April 7, 1948. The single-stall wooden locomotive shed was razed within a year or so of this date as the diesels would have all mechanical work done at Middletown, and any inspections and minor servicing needed at this place would be done outside in the weather. Later plans for a new engine-house did not get beyond the drawing board. For the most part, diesels used new or rebuilt factory parts that were kept by the stores department at the main shop whereas most of the parts for steam locomotives were cut, stamped and forged as needed. Dieselization therefore did much to centralize locomotive maintenance.—JOHN PICKETT.

As viewed from the caboose of an arriving train at Cadosia, the 123 attends to tasks against the beautiful backdrop of Hawk Mountain. To the left are foundation stones of the coaling tower. The distant signal's semaphore blades indicate a clear passage through Hawk Mountain Tunnel for any immediate southbounds. Just beyond the distant curve was South Yard and the remnants of a coal-storage facility—MARV COHEN.

haust gases high enough to avoid their being drawn into the cab.

Early and middle SWl and NW2 production (not to be confused with the previously mentioned "early" and "late" locomotives) had a flat "transition" section between the cab and the taper coming down from the top of the engine hood; later production had only the taper. The sides of the engine hood also tapered inward where they joined the cab. These three angled surfaces provided increased visibility for the locomotive crew.

The General Steel Castings (GRS) truck, the so-called AAR (Association of American Railroads) type A or "rigid" truck, was used under the NW2's and was used by virtually all diesel switcher manufacturers although not on all models. These trucks had friction bearings and drop equalizers. According to engine crews, they did not provide as smooth a ride as the Blomberg trucks used under road units.

The NW2 used a V-12 version of EMD's 567 engine which produced 1,000 h.p. and originally powered a D4D generator. The 567A was substituted near the end of the war as was the 600-volt D15A generator. Current flowed to four D-7 traction motors which could be connected in series for low speed and heavy tractive effort or in series-parallel for higher-speed operation. As with the F3's, the purchaser had the choice of manual or automatic transition for making these electrical connections.

By the time NW2 production began, EMC was producing its own electrical gear and the switcher shared a host of components and accessories with FT and F3 road diesels. This included power assemblies (pistons, cylinder liners and heads), electrical gear and gear ratios. Since the production covered a ten-year period—minus the 1942-1945 ban—upgraded parts were available for retrofitting to earlier units.

NW2's were 44 feet, 5 inches long between coupling faces, carried 600 gallons of fuel and rode on 40-inch wheels. Loaded weight was 250,000 pounds and starting tractive effort was 62,500 pounds. Like the GE 44-tonner and the F3, the NW2 went through a number of production phases which were marked by both mechanical and carbody changes. The latter were usually subtle, such as the number and placement of louvers, type of headlight and several small frame and superstructure details. All phases employed a single belt-driven fan to draw engine cooling air in through front shutters. It was then forced through roof-mounted radiators and exhausted out through louvers that covered the forward top of the hood. By the time of the O&W order, NW2's were equipped with automatic temperature control which opened and closed the shutters admitting air to the radiators. This system kept the engine water temperature between 155 and 165 degrees.

The O&W's NW2's

O&W officials vacillated for some time on whether to order all NW2's or to substitute a few SW1's. It was thought that four SW1's would be better suited for certain jobs and this would also save some money on the initial order. This savings, however, would limit flexibility by requiring assigned locomotives to some locations, and it was finally decided to go back to the original plan of ordering only NW2's.

The O&W paid $2,009,133 ($95,673 each) for it's 21 NW2's. (Financing is discussed in more detail in the F3 chapter as the NW2's were part of the F3 road diesel order and were also primarily financed by the equipment trust of 1947.) They entered the roster as they were received in groups in 1948. Company records indicate that the units were delivered by the NYC at Oneida, N.Y., the D&H at Carbondale, Pa., and one came to Middletown via the Erie. Unlike the road units, the NW2's inability to operate at maximum road speeds precluded their working east in road service, hence O&W had to pay over $20,000 in shipping charges. Each unit had the same 65:12 gear ratio as O&W's FT's, however this did not allow them to operate at the higher speeds of the F units.

While negotiating with EMD for the units, the O&W did inquire about multiple-unit controls

The iron horse had fully assumed a new character and personality along all reaches of the O&W by mid-1948, when this scene of the 118 was recorded at Delhi. Bright colors and new sounds replaced the hissing, smoking, black steamers that arrived in Delhi each day. The operational pattern was the same but the chant of two-cycle internal combustion, its bluish-gray exhaust smoke, and the flat, single note of its horn are what announced the O&W's presence for the remaining years of its service to the community.
—JOHN PICKETT.

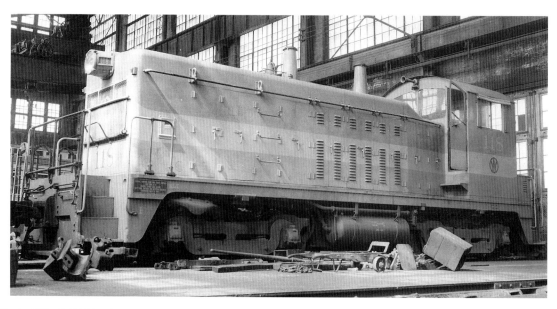

The date is March 24, 1957—five days before the end—and we're at Middletown shops. A mechanical representative of the New York Central will soon subject the 118 to a thorough examination. The unit will be judged sound, papers will be signed and the 118 will leave Middletown for wider travels on the far-flung NYC system as their 9503—JOHN D. HAHN JR.

Led by the 120 (apparently being operated by O&W management) nine of the 19 NW2's sold to NYC have arrived at Kingston, N.Y., and are being switched over to the former Ulster & Delaware tracks for interchange in April 1957. For the most part, these units went to work at points in eastern New York State. The NYC must have been power hungry since they immediately went to work without a change of number or color.—ROBERT HAINES.

and engine heating systems that could be used during layover periods. Multiple-unit control, as a $369 per-unit extra, seems to have been refused as a cost-saving measure—and there had to be times when O&W later questioned that decision. EMD offered both electrical and oil-fueled heating systems, but apparently the O&W also did not consider this to be worth the expense and it was not applied.

EMD told the railroad that the NW2's should not be expected to give satisfactory service in road use at speeds above 35 m.p.h. as severe rough riding and shimmying would result. EMD did suggest that the O&W consider the

application of field shunt contactors, at an additional cost of $333 per unit, to permit a one-third increase in speed when operating over the main line. Interestingly, these devices were applied. The operating manual issued to O&W engineers indicated that the NW2's could be operated at 50 mph although EMD recommended 45 mph as the speed limit for the type A truck. Apparently, O&W officials believed—initially, anyway—that speed was only a function of gear ratio and that the 65:12 ratio of the switchers as well as the 40-inch wheels would make them equal to the FT's (and F3's) in road speed. But the key was in the NW2 electrical system,

which was designed for tonnage, not speed.

These NW2's had only two possible electrical connections between the generator and traction motors when the unit was going forward. Unlike the road units, the NW's did have automatic transition, which made them easier to operate. One option, however, allowed the engineer to forestall transition to series-parallel by pressing a switch labeled IN-SERIES. This was necessary if the locomotive was to be used in heavy switching or when frequent reverse operation was required.

The NW2's were painted in the color scheme established by the FT's, but with some modification to the pattern of the yellow stripe so that it could pass above the battery box and across the rear of the cab. Affixed on the radiator screen of each unit was a 22-inch diameter red O&W emblem cut from sheet steel. Another customized addition to these units were pairs of marker or classification lamps that had come from retired steam locomotives. A push-pole, used to push cars on parallel tracks, hung over the rear truck on the engineer's side. In use, the pole was placed between poling pockets located on car and locomotive corners. Since the poles sometimes splintered and hands were crushed in placing them, it was a dangerous practice and has since been outlawed.

There wasn't a single foot of main or branchline track that the NW's didn't work. They idled many a lonely hour at the remote reaches of the system as well as gathered in clusters at Middletown, Cadosia, Norwich and Mayfield, which seemed to host the largest number with as many as five units working the yard, mine runs and an occasional trip to the Lehigh Valley at Coxton. One of the more unusual NW2 assignments was the handling of trains SU-1 and US-2 between Norwich and Canal Branch Yard in Utica, probably because low speed limits kept the FT's and the later F3's from being utilized to maximum advantage.

(ABOVE) A former O&W locomotive on former O&W tracks: UV 113, nee O&W 113, does local work at Mount Upton, N.Y., in 1958. The O&W sold this line (the New Berlin Branch) to the Unadilla Valley in 1941. H. E. Salzberg Co. owned the UV and was believed to be interested in purchasing and operating the Sidney-Norwich part of the O&W after the line shut down. Apparently for this purpose, UV bought O&W 111-113 with this last unit being painted in the road's trademark cream and orange. The three units retained their O&W numbers on the UV. When the expansion failed to take place, the UV found them surplus, and they eventually wound up on the CRI&P.—JIM SHAUGHNESSY.
(BELOW) Rock Island 796 was O&W 112.—WAYNE SITTNER COLLECTION.

6/The EMD F3's

As an important defense supplier during World War II, EMD had learned much from the way its products successfully responded to the high demands on both the home and battle fronts. The tremendous pressures that the war years had placed upon EMD's first road diesels had proven the company's mechanical and electrical concepts to be sound, and the impressive dollar savings over steam operations made the diesels even more appealing.

Delayed modernization programs and war profits saw many railroads that had been on the brink of ambitious projects before the war started finally bringing new technology to customers. Along with other locomotive builders, Electro-Motive was anticipating a postwar boom in the dieselization of America's railroads. It prepared for it by developing improved road diesel locomotives and expanding the LaGrange (Ill.) facility to produce up to 100 locomotives per month. The company soon found these steps to be inad-equate to meet the demand.

Production of an advanced model F-unit was about to begin even as O&W's FT's were leaving the plant. A further-refined 567 engine, the 567-B, was developed for the new design, to be known as the F3. Other improvements on the FT's successor included the elimination of the belt drives, which were expensive and time-consuming to maintain. EMD returned to electrically driven accessories using an alternator, integral with the main generator, to power induction motors that turned engine cooling fans and traction-motor blowers. Since these appliances were no longer mechanically driven, design engineers had greater freedom in locating them in the crowded engine room.

Piping and wiring arrangements were simplified for easier installation and access. The electrical cabinet was relocated to the back of the cab for greater accessibility. A more-compact engine-room setup provided more space for a steam generator on units intended for passenger service.

(FACING PAGE) Through New York Central's four-track West Shore territory south of Dumont, N.J., locomotive 501 powers the Weehawken-bound, nine-car consist of train 4 circa 1949. O&W's three 500-series F3A's, units 501-503, often saw passenger duties, although they were not equipped with steam generators nor did they have a "passenger" gear ratio that allowed them to sprint any faster than their 800-class brethren. But, a single F3 worked just fine for the leisurely schedules of O&W passenger runs, even when they were heavily laden with travelers, as was the case here. Since O&W owned scant passenger equipment, most if not all the cars on summer trains were leased, usually from NYC, although the third car out in No. 4 on this day is a Lackawanna coach. The New York State Thruway, a four-lane Route 17 and a less-than-two-hour trip to the Catskills by car did not yet exist, so many vacationers still depended upon the O&W to take them "upstate."—JOHN KRAUSE.

(ABOVE AND ABOVE RIGHT) With all roof openings covered to keep out the elements, F3 502 stands ready for delivery at EMD's LaGrange facility in 1948. In a few days, the 502 will arrive in Middletown and aid in the displacement of the last of O&W's venerable steam engines—an occasion that will be sadly noted by many. Engine crew attire will reflect the lack of soot and cinders as white caps (usually reserved for electric-locomotive motormen) and sport shirts replace striped Kromer caps, Sweet-Orrs and bib overalls.—COURTESY EMD.

Apparently there were problems with the new generator, and until they could be resolved, the same generator used in the FT had to be used in the new locomotive, limiting it to the same 1350 h.p. per unit of the FT. Thus, until the generator problem was resolved, the F3 designation was temporarily shelved and the new model became known as the F2, serving as a transition between the FT and the F3. The F2 had a production run of about one year, and it did reasonably well in sales, with over 100 units sold to eight roads.

On Oct. 22, 1946, coincident with the 10th anniversary of its LaGrange plant, EMD unveiled the F3. (Production is believed to actually have begun earlier since EMD said that 30 roads had already placed orders.) The F3 was essentially the F2 with the improved 600-volt main generator that better utilized the inherent horsepower of the 567 engine. The F3 was thus rated at 1500 h.p., a gain of 150 h.p. over the F2 and FT.

A four-unit, 6000-h.p. A-B-B-A F3 demonstrator set toured the country and was hosted by more than 25 railroads, possibly including the O&W. (One source says that two demonstrator sets, one geared for passenger and the other for freight service, were on tour).

In common with the FT, the F3 used a truss arrangement to carry the weight of the diesel prime mover, generator and auxiliaries. Welded construction with reinforcing plates was used throughout the body. The nose was formed of curved stampings which were welded together, and the sides were covered with metal paneling secured by battens that allowed for some torsional flexing without buckling. The cab interior was lined with sound-absorbing material, and the wood floor was covered with linoleum. An unverified report from an engineer on the Pennsylvania Railroad claimed that the window crank handles on PRR's new F3's matched those of his GMC car!

Although the F2/F3 followed the general silhouette of an FT, the new F-unit line broke from that model in many external features as well as internal improvements. F3 A-units were 50 feet, 8 inches over coupler pulling faces compared with 48 feet, 3 inches for the FT. F3B's were 50 feet while the FTB was 48 feet, 3 inches. Gone were the four porthole windows of the FT's, and variations of two or three widely spaced portholes characterized the F3.

(ABOVE RIGHT) The engineer's side of the F3 cab. The engineer here appears to be watching his ammeter as he operates the transition lever. Many F3's were delivered with automatic transition, but O&W's units had to be compatible with the FT's and therefore retained manual transition. (ABOVE LEFT) The left side of the F3 cab was stark simplicity. Note the "glove boxes" which probably contained waste rags and pads of the maintenance forms that were filled in after each trip.—BOTH PHOTOS, WALTER RICH COLLECTION. (BELOW) The back of the engineer's seat has been folded down so we can see most of the instruments and controls of an F3. The large dial at the upper left is the speedometer and speed recorder. To its right is the ammeter and transition indicator. Above this and to the left is the PCS (pneumatic control switch) light which indicates a "penalty" or emergency brake application. The three similar gauges (visible between the the two brake handles) are (left to right) main and equalizing reservoir pressure gauge, brake pipe and brake cylinder air gauge and sup- pression pipe air gauge. To the right of these is a circular EMD medallion. The two lights above the gauges are the dy- namic brake warning and the wheel-slip indicator lights. At the lower left of the speedometer is the transition and dy- namic brake control, next to it and "pointing" to the right is the throttle. The horizontal, rectangular opening below is where the removable reverser handle goes and it sits on the stand just above the opening. The short handle below the three gauges is the independent brake and the large handle over two of them is the train brake. To the immediate right of the independent brake handle is the air valve for the bell.—HANK TREGER.

(ABOVE) Back-to-back A units (503-501) negotiate a double-slip switch at NYC's Weehawken (N.J.) West Shore terminal. The date of the photograph is Sept. 7, 1953, and this set may have worked the final Labor Day weekend passenger trips. The tan three-story building above the 503 housed West Shore dispatchers.—DAVID CONNOR. (RIGHT) Three coaches and F3 503 arrive at the passenger terminal in Weehawken. A tunnel brought the double-track main line through the Palisades escarpment that forms the backdrop. The terminal tracks, platform and ferry-house made for a tight fit between the rock wall and the Hudson River. —HARRY ZANNIE PHOTO COURTESY OF CHET STEITZ.

Originally, the illuminated number boxes on the nose of the F3 were very similar to those of the FT, but in later phases they were enlarged and mounted at a 45-degree angle for improved locomotive identification by line-side operating personnel. Although this was a sensible change, it forever marred the otherwise clean appearance of the EMD nose on later F3's and all following models.

The semi-permanent drawbar coupling of the FT's was discarded and most, if not all, railroads chose the flexibility of having couplers on both ends of their F2's and F3's. The asymmetry of truck spacing readily visible on the FT was hardly noticeable on F3 A-units since there was only an 8-inch difference (the front truck was 10 feet, 8 inches in and the rear truck was an even 10 feet in from the end of the car body) and on the B units, trucks were equally spaced. (FT's had a very noticeable overhang since the A-unit front truck was well recessed behind the pilot and the B-unit's rear truck center was 11 feet, 9 inches in from the rear of car body.) The greater length between truck centers and equal frame overhang beyond the trucks gave the F3's a more balanced appearance. Like their FT brethren, F3's had the same 40-inch wheels and a 1200-gallon fuel tank.

As with the GE 44-tonners, the F3's had a number of details that were specific to certain periods or phases of construction. For example, later F3 phases, including those of the O&W, had four additional air intakes along the sides between the windows of the A units, apparently to increase the amount of air available for engine aspiration—a hypothesis supported by the fact that F3 B-units did not have these air intakes since their regular intakes extended through what would have been the "cab" end of the unit. Final F3 and the succeeding model F7 production had louvers over the A-unit intakes, presumably to protect against wind-driven precipitation soaking into the filter elements.

All radiator cores on the F3 were grouped together over the engine, and thus the four rooftop radiator fans were joined in one line rather than in groups of two as on the FT. The cooling fans could be operated in any required number to meet cooling needs and in various combinations to equalize motor wear. On the FT's, these fans were flush with the rooftop, while on the F3's they stood above the roof line. The height of these fans depended upon the motor used to power them.

Later, railroads cross-matched parts from different phases and later F-unit models, and many F3's had a mix of both high and low fans (all O&W units had the low "pan-top" fans). The radiator air-intake shutters were thermostatically controlled which kept the engine temperature within a narrower range than was possible with the old manual shutters. The reduced expansion and contraction of engine parts, provided more uniform performance, and reduced the possibility of fluid leakage.

The dynamic-brake resistor grids and their blower motors were redesigned to be a complete sub-assembly that would neatly "plug-in" through a roof hatch if a railroad had requested

There are plenty of pictures of O&W passenger trains at Roscoe, and it's no wonder. From 1948 to the end of passenger service in 1953, Roscoe was the northern terminus for O&W passenger service. The trains were conveniently scheduled for a one-day Weehawken-Roscoe round trip, and the layover time at "RK" allowed for lunch and a few photographs before boarding for the return trip. During such an outing on Sept. 5, 1953, David Connor found the 502 on train 2 with a consist of baggage-RPO and three West Shore suburban coaches. The depot area is now the site of the Roscoe Railroad Museum which features a display of O&W items and photographs housed in a former Erie caboose and a museum building across the street.—DAVID CONNOR.

the dynamic-brake feature. Two rectangular, longitudinal, screened openings permitted the heated air from the resistor grids to escape. Gone were the boxy housings and longitudinal louvers of the FT's dynamics, as all air came in through the sides.

The electro-pneumatic governor of the FT was replaced by one of electro-hydraulic design. This provided better synchronization between the engine speed and the loading of the traction motors and also improved synchronization between units operating in multiple.

The F3 also introduced automatic transition, an option the O&W declined since it could not have been used when F3's were operated in multiple with FT's. For roads like O&W, which opted for manual transition, a new easier-to-understand transition meter had been developed for F2/F3 production.

One of the F3's greatest advantages over the FT was that it could be retrofitted with a number of upgraded components. Many of these were small parts or auxiliary equipment that made for more economical operation and maintenance of EMD units. One example of this was EMD's discontinued use of organic insulation materials for traction motors. New silicon- and glass-based insulating materials, developed during the war,

were better able to resist deterioration by heat and moisture. As such newer technology (much of it the result of wartime shortages and substitutions) found its way into peacetime uses, retrofits were made available.

The "building block" concept of assigning diesel units in multiple to make a locomotive set that was tailored to a specific job or operating conditions had been introduced earlier, but not until the F3 did the practice really take hold. FT operation was essentially limited to 2700- or 5400-h.p. combinations unless a road had replaced all drawbars with couplers. (Many of the roads that did this did so only after experience with F3 operation.) EMD initially said that "up to four units" could be operated in multiple, but railroads soon began exceeding that number.

In promoting the F3, EMD made use of the slogan "28 in 1," apparently referring to the number of ways a four-unit locomotive set could be tailored for different uses by multiplying four by the seven gear ratios that were offered for the model. EMD emphasized the ease with which an F3's gearing could be changed for seasonal and other operational assignments; e.g., a summer passenger unit could be regeared for slower, winter helper service on a mountain division.

(BELOW) A four-unit set of F3's and FT's have brought a freight from Sibley Junction down the Lehigh Valley's Austin Branch and into Coxton Yard at Pittston, Pa. Having cleared the Austin Junction switch, the crew will shove the train back into LV's yard where the westbound cars will be added to a Buffalo-bound LV train. The diesels are crossing the Lackawanna River which joins the North Branch of the Susquehanna at this point. —ED MILLER.

During a cab ride on a Cadosia-bound freight led by an F3, the photographer used the distinctive EMD cab-unit windshield to frame the picturesque Lakewood (Pa.) depot on the downgrade between Starlight and Poyntelle. The order board is clear in our direction, but out for opposing trains. The signal was serving the purpose of manual-block protection for the movement of the train.—WALTER RICH COLLECTION.

O&W's F3's

It was both the court's and management's hope that the O&W would be completely dieselized in as short a period of time as possible. All those connected with O&W affairs, however, must have known that wartime shortages and priorities would hinder the railroad's ability to do so. Financing continued to be difficult to arrange, yet the road needed to realize the savings that fully dieselized operations would provide. The best that could be done in 1945 was to obtain the nine FT sets, and although the railroad did achieve significant savings with partial dieselization, it still had to maintain facilities that accommodated steam power.

Although the initial dieselization studies were introduced and pressed forward by Lyford, the completion of the program was up to his successors after he left the O&W in 1944. The critical through-freight service between Mayfield and the Maybrook connections was essentially dieselized with the FT's as was a major part of the Mayfield-Utica run. Nonetheless, virtually all road switching and most yard, passenger, milk and secondary freight operations were still under the reins of steam.

A high level of internal correspondence as well as continued communication with Electro-Motive regarding additional diesel power is evident in a "paper trail" found in several collections of O&W information. Before O&W could resume the march toward complete dieseliza-

tion, the original plan had to be re-evaluated in regard to the needs of the O&W, its experience with the FT's, and EMD's continued development and improvement of models.

On June 5, 1946, trustees Gebhardt and Sieghardt petitioned the bankruptcy court for permission to purchase 27 additional diesel locomotives. The initial request was for two 2700-h.p. and two 1500-h.p. freight locomotives* and 23 1000-h.p. switching locomotives. The cost was figured to be $2.6 million, but a further savings of $860,000 per year (in addition to savings realized with the FT's) was anticipated once the final steam locomotive was removed from service.

Despite the flurry of activity, no formal order was signed due to the uncertainty of a pending adjustment of claims for back wages by both operating and non-operating employees. There was also concern about the effect of labor strikes, primarily in coal, upon the road's income. (Some delays were caused by the O&W's changes in locomotive options and in model selection as well as EMD's already-full production schedule to fill earlier orders from other roads).

Not until October 1947 did O&W trustees return to the court asking to proceed on the loan. On Nov. 14, the court approved the petition to make application to the ICC for permission to seek another RFC loan. A letter from EMD,

---

*The request for two 2700-h.p. units must be a reference to FT's, but they were no longer being produced. EMD no doubt made this clear as soon as it was contacted.

dated Nov. 5, 1947, confirmed the final details of the purchase: two 3000-h.p. A-B F3 sets, three 1500-h.p. F3 A units and 21 NW2 switchers. On Dec. 1, 1947, the "New York, Ontario & Western Equipment Trust of 1947" for $2.6 million was issued and purchased by the RFC, while the Central Hanover Bank & Trust Company was again designated equipment trustee. In their loan application, the trustees emphasized their belief that full dieselization was the key to a profitable operation.

"There is a manifest need for the continued operation of this railroad system. Many communities are served thereby which have no other railroad facility and they would be subjected to grievous hardship and damage by the cessation of operation of this railroad property. Any such result is entirely unnecessary, since it can be made to live and serve as a self-sustaining, reorganized entity if it is permitted to effect complete dieselization of its power. Without such dieselization, there is a serious question whether or not disintegration and liquidation of the property can be prevented."

The new trust had essentially the same wording as the equipment trust of 1945 but was to reach maturity on Dec. 1, 1957. By the time all the paperwork and permission had been secured and the exact models and numbers finalized, the cost of the locomotives had risen to $3,081,535 for which the RFC loan would pay almost 85 percent.

(ABOVE) F3's and FT's display a spirit of teamwork as they roar into Campbell Hall—the gateway to Maybrook Yard—with an southbound symbol train out of Scranton.—T. J. DONOHUE. (RIGHT) Once often assigned to passenger duties, F3A 503 is shown working with A-B FT set 802 at Cadosia on March 17, 1957, making for a somewhat uncommon (on the O&W) A-B-A locomotive set. Originally purchased to operate singly in local freight service, the 503 was quickly displaced by the more-suitable NW2's. However, the footboards and grab irons remained though out the O&W careers of all three 500-series locomotives.—JOHN D. HAHN Jr.

A passenger special, perhaps an officers' inspection train, sits in the siding at the north end of Middletown station. The trustees, department heads, officials, shippers and just about anyone else who might affect the outcome of reorganization would be invited to ride such trains. Since these inspection trips took two or more days to complete, meal and overnight accommodations would usually be arranged in on-line towns since O&W did not have dining or sleeping cars.—MARV COHEN.

The Heater Cars

THE CANCELLATION OF STEAM GENERATORS in the F-unit orders meant that the railroad had to devise some other manner of heating its passenger trains in cold weather if they, too, were to be dieselized. The answer was to build two steam-generator cars, HT-1 and HT-2, constructed from two original X-class 2-10-2 tenders. Through extending the tender sides upward and curving them over to form the roof, the heater cars had a superstructure that matched, in cross-section, a diesel body. In fact, they were painted to match the diesels.

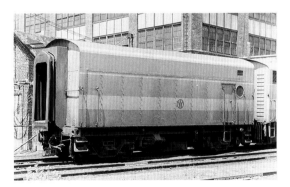

Built by Middletown shops in May 1948, the HT-1, with its Vapor-Clarkson steam generator innards, generated 1,600 pounds of steam per hour at 250 pounds pressure. The car was 30 feet, 2 inches long, just over 14 feet high and carried 6,000 gallons of water and 600 gallons of fuel. It cost $19,389.88 to construct—considerably more than the steam-generator option in the original F3 orders! HT-2, very similar in appearance, was constructed in May 1949.

The F3's were equipped with controls for operating the heater cars. Since no photographs have appeared that show FT's in winter passenger service, they apparently were not wired to work with this equipment. A number of dispatchers' diaries also indicate steam locomotives were used in passenger service through the winter of 1947-48, steam's final winter on the O&W.

The "HT" designation, of course, stood for "heater tender," but they were also known as "coffee pots," "tea kettles," "steam-heater cars" and other aptly suitable names. The O&W was not alone in employing steam-generator cars to help keep passengers warm. New York Central, Rio Grande, Great Northern and even Amtrak employed such vehicles, some of which, like the O&W, were built from steam-locomotive tenders.

With the end of year-round passenger service in 1950, the heater cars had little further purpose. The HT-2 was sold in August 1953 to the Fernwood, Columbia & Gulf for $3,750 while the HT-1 remained on the final roster, probably on standby to provide heat for passenger cars on inspection trips in cold weather. Along with a number of well-worn freight cars, cabooses, seven FT sets and tons of shop machinery, it passed many years in storage and is believed to have been scrapped at Tappan, N.Y. in 1970.—R.M.

The Reconstruction Finance Corporation

THE RECONSTRUCTION FINANCE CORPORATION *was authorized by Congress in January 1932 to provide interim government financing for existing financial, agricultural, and industrial enterprises that were otherwise unable to obtain financing or investment capital under reasonable terms. At the time, the American economy was in a deep depression, with commercial activity, prices, wages and asset values in steady decline. The RFC was one of several Depression-era "alphabet agencies" established to stimulate employment and create a better degree of economic stability.*

In his book, FIFTY BILLION DOLLARS: MY THIRTEEN YEARS WITH THE RFC, *Jessie Jones, chairman of RFC's board of directors, claimed that of the 250,000 miles of U.S. railroad trackage, more than one-third entered receivership or bankruptcy during the depression of the 1930's, and another third would have done so were it not for RFC loans or other assistance. The RFC lent more than a billion dollars to 89 railroads to finance purchase of new equipment, refinance maturing debt, pay interest on existing bonds, pay taxes or provide working capital. Under the law, the RFC could lend money to a railroad only after the Interstate Commerce Commission had certified that the line could continue to meet its obligations and avoid reorganization or bankruptcy. By taking collateral to secure the loans, RFC hoped to eventually recover its money even if a bankruptcy occurred subsequent to loan disbursement.*

As the Depression continued, the railroads' situation mirrored the overall economic decline; hundreds of thousands of railroad workers had been laid off, maintenance expenses drastically reduced, and new equipment purchases postponed. In the spring of 1938, Congress amended the RFC Act to permit loans for new railroad equipment purchases (with the equipment as collateral) as well as loans to finance the rehire of former rail workers—regardless of the financial condition of the borrower.

The preferred method for new equipment was the issuance of equipment trust notes. An equipment trust is a device that allows railroads to finance the installment purchase of locomotives and rolling stock. Until the final payment is made, title to the equipment is held by a trustee for the benefit of the note holders. The RFC purchased equipment trust certificates for many railroads, with various banks acting as trustees to collect payments from the borrowers and remit them to the note holders. After payments remained current for several years, the RFC was often able to sell the equipment trust notes to financial institutions or other investors.

As the RFC grew, it assumed increasing responsibility for disbursing huge sums of money, and although it was an independent agency that was exempt by law from political considerations, political and private lobbying to influence the agency's business judgments also increased. Once the Republicans came to power in January 1953, they moved rapidly to liquidate the RFC, which, although a Depression-era agency, had remained in business after the nation's return to prosperity. In September 1953 its lending authority was terminated and in June 1957 the RFC was abolished and its remaining functions were transferred to other federal agencies.—ROGER COOK.

(FACING PAGE) At milepost 142 near Cooks Falls, N.Y., on April 15, 1948, brand-new F3's 821 and 822, bringing train NE-6 south, struck a boulder and derailed. It was said that the damage was severe enough to require that the units be returned to EMD for repairs. Photographer Patorskey's vantage point of the mishap was from across the East Branch of the Delaware River—BOB PASTORSKEY.

Ironically, these delays contributed a shortage of motive power, and the railroad had to restore a number of retired steam engines (whose flue time had not expired) to service. In addition, steam locomotives were leased from the New Haven, Jersey Central and D&H (the D&H engine, a Camelback 2-8-0, was subsequently purchased for $7,500 in October 1947). A small number of Whitcomb center-cab switchers were also leased from one or more equipment dealers.

The F3's rolled into Middletown in March 1948. It appeared that the two A-B sets (821A&B and 822A&B), which cost $301,701 each, were intended for passenger service since steam generators had originally been specified for both B units. However, the final specifications had eliminated the steam generators and requested dynamic brakes on all four units. Approximately $13,000 per unit was saved by dropping the steam generators. Also, since it did not show in any of the specifications noted, it appears the B units were not equipped with hostler controls, handy for individual movement in terminal areas. Each 230-ton A-B set (both A and B units had couplers at both ends) exerted 115,000 pounds of tractive effort.

All the F3's were equipped with 65:12 gearing for multiple-unit operation with the FT's as well as for the lower speed and greater power that the O&W's route required. This gear ratio was an extra cost option because it required special traction motors with integral 12-tooth pinion armature shafts.

The three 500-series F3's, costing $157,000 each, also entered the roster in March 1948. Two of the three units were to have steam generators, and none were to be equipped with dynamic brakes, but as with the 800's, the units were delivered sans steam generators and with dynamic brakes. Each 115-ton unit exerted 57,500 pounds tractive effort.

The F3's paint scheme was a close match to that of the FT's, with minor differences. Numbers were not painted under the headlight nor did the F3's receive the "Rayflector" number plates on the nose door.

All of the F3's, except for the 503, worked their way east to the O&W at Maybrook. One of the first assignments these units handled was the Delhi way freight, which has led to the belief that the F3's were to be used as road-switchers. Although this seems like an unusual assignment for a cab unit today, it should be remembered that EMD had only just begun road-switcher production about the time these F3's were delivered, and that, back then, any dieselized service—regardless of locomotive model used—was considered superior to the same operation with steam power. It probably did not take long, though, before crews made it clear to management that an NW2 was indeed better suited to road switching runs such as the Delhi job.

O&W made some of its own modifications to the F3 fleet. For example, because the three 500-series F3's were intended to operate singly in local service, Middletown shops applied footboards to both ends of all three 500's. In addition, a long, single handrail was installed on all the F3 noses for use by hostlers and shop workers.

It was not uncommon for O&W to m.u. its FT's and F3's, but it took a special m.u. transition jumper cable, carried aboard all F3's, to do the job. F3's had a 27-point m.u. connection while FT's had 21 points. Combining, say, a single F3 with an A-B FT provided a 4200-h.p. locomotive set that added a greater degree of flexibility to the roster. None of the O&W's A units had m.u. receptacles on the nose, a feature many surrounding roads began applying to their units in the late 1950's.

Although it was possible, neither photographs nor written records confirm that O&W ever assembled a locomotive set consisting of two FT's bracketing one or both F3B units. Photographs also seem to indicate that the F3's were not frequently found on the north end of the railroad. Their greater reliability served a better purpose when assigned to the time-sensitive manifests on the Mayfield-Maybrook runs.

Probably because they frequently appear in passenger service in numerous photographs, many believe the 500's were purchased for that service. However, correspondence between the railroad and EMD refers to the three as freight locomotives. Still, a single 500 class was an ideal

The Proposed Equipment Trust of 1949

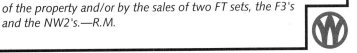

CENTRAL HANOVER BANK AND TRUST COMPANY
NEW YORK, N. Y.
TRUSTEE, OWNER AND LESSOR,
NEW YORK, ONTARIO AND WESTERN RAILWAY
EQUIPMENT TRUST OF 1949

UNTIL THE END OF MAY 1949, the O&W had been meeting the required payments of the three equipment trusts that had made it possible for the railroad to dieselize. Unfortunately, because of declining earnings, the railroad defaulted on the scheduled payments after that date on both the 1945 and 1947 trusts. Meetings with RFC officials resulted in a revised payment schedule. A plan was formulated to consolidate the trusts into a new issue to be named, "New York, Ontario & Western Railway Equipment Trust of 1949." Work on this plan went as far as making new trust plates (ABOVE) which would have replaced those applied in 1945 and 1948, however the consolidated trust plan was never carried out. According to newspaper and company records, the RFC attempted to seize the diesels early in the 1950's when the railroad again defaulted on the loan. However it was unsuccessful and at the time of O&W's closure, $1,978,000 was still outstanding on the diesel trusts of 1945 and 1947. Its possible the remaining balance was reduced by the liquidation of the property and/or by the sales of two FT sets, the F3's and the NW2's.—R.M.

(TOP) The 822 peers out at a world that, for it, has radically changed. It is April 19, 1957, and the O&W has been shut down, but every few days a hostler shows up to start the locomotive, charge the batteries and move it a few feet. A good wipe-down has removed road grime from the body so potential buyers get an impression of a well-cared-for locomotive. Within a year the four 800-series F3's would wear Erie black and yellow and pass near some of their old haunts in the service of their new owners.—ROBERT F. COLLINS. (ABOVE) The acquisition of O&W 821 and 822 (A and B units) increased Erie's F3 roster to 45 units. Here is former 821A&B, with new numbers and paint, at Corning, N.Y.—JOHN D. HAHN JR.

unit for O&W's off-season passenger trains. A self-contained steam-generator car (converted from a steam locomotive tender), a milk car or two, an RPO-baggage and a couple of coaches were well within the unit's ability to hold to the schedule. Use of a single 1500-h.p. F3 avoided employing a 2700-h.p. FT set better suited for heavier duties.

The complete dieselization of road trains meant the end of one time-honored practice: fire patrols. During the fall season, or any dry period in which conditions were favorable for forest fires, the railroad's section gangs were required to patrol its routes after the passage of a steam-powered train to ensure that neither sparks dropping from the ashpan nor hot cinders set brush or forest fires along the right-of-way. Despite this precaution, fires still occurred occasionally, and the railroad had to pay for the resulting damage. Although diesels were not completely innocent of this problem, they significantly reduced the chances of fire and made fire patrols unnecessary.

When diesels came to the O&W, they brought with them a strong belief in their ability to not simply haul tonnage efficiently, but to also haul a railroad back on its feet. Future research may prove that dieselization was the single most significant effort that kept the railroad alive after 1937. If so, those of us so intrigued by the New York, Ontario & Western will understand that they also drew it closer in time, word and imagery to us of the present day.

(TOP) F3 503 has nosed its way into Scranton with a passenger Extra comprised of a heater car, an old baggage-RPO and two O&W coach-observation cars. The train paused long enough at Park Place depot (behind the orange box car) for photographer Cohen—a passenger aboard the special—to scramble up the hillside for this overview. Later in the trip (ABOVE), the train halts at an unidentified siding. Marv leaned out from the rear platform of one of the two observation cars to catch two crewmen walking forward while the train waited for its meet with a freight.—BOTH PHOTOS, MARV COHEN.

7/Curious Diesel Doings

From an enigmatic notation in an employees' timetable concerning the passage of Erie F7's through Liberty, N.Y., to the photographic evidence of American Car & Foundry's Talgo train in Middletown, there were several ordinary and extraordinary diesel visitors on the O&W. These appearances must have made lineside observers do a double take, and for employees, they broke the ordinary routine of passing gray-and-yellow locomotives.

The Train of Tomorrow

In the December 1985 issue of *Passenger Train Journal*, Karl Zimmermann reported the history of an unusual traveling sales tool: "The *Train of Tomorrow*, handsome in blue-green dress with stainless-steel trim, was born of a collaboration among Pullman-Standard design engineers, Electro-Motive engineers and stylists from GM's Detroit plants." Focal point of the new state-of-the-art streamliner were its four dome cars—a dome coach, dome diner, dome sleeper and dome-lounge observation. Powering the "vest-pocket" domeliner was an EMD E7, a distant cousin to the F-unit.

The *Train of Tomorrow* unveiled a new dimension in rail travel and gave promise of a new era in passenger comfort. The experimental train prepared the railroads to fight highways and airways to protect their passenger-hauling supremacy once production lines had been realigned for peacetime production after World War II.

The demonstration train was to arouse public interest and bring in orders from the railroads. All a railroad had to do to host the train was provide a few display sites and let the GM-Pullman Standard consortium do the rest.

In May 1947, the *Train of Tomorrow* made its inaugural run, from Chicago to French Lick, Ind., on the Monon. From there the consist went on exhibition tours totaling 65,000 miles in addition to being displayed at the Chicago Railroad Fair in 1948-49. The train came to the O&W via the Lackawanna at Scranton and probably was open for inspection at several on-line points before it appearance at Wickham Avenue in Middletown. The extent of the *Train of Tomorrow*'s tour over the O&W is thus far unknown, but we surmise that O&W tunnels must have presented some tight clearances.

Of course, we know there were no sales in Middletown—nor did domes come to any railroads in the greater Northeastern U.S. outside of the Baltimore & Ohio, at least not in the postwar days—but one wonders what was going through the minds of people on the platform as they viewed this marvel of modern transportation on their local road.

New Haven Alco PA's

American Locomotive Company's diesel locomotive assembly facility was located in Schenectady, N.Y., and one of its major customers in the Northeast was the New Haven Railroad. Records show NYNH&H 0772 as one of a second order for PA passenger units assembled in 1949 and delivered via the Delaware & Hudson to Sidney and O&W to Maybrook Yard. It's likely that the other units of this order, not to mention other Alco models—DL109's, RS's, FA's and all the switchers—followed the same routing to the New Haven. After all, the New Haven was a major shareholder of O&W common stock, and it would behoove the New Haven to use railroads in which it had a vested interest.

Leased Whitcomb Switchers

A number of Whitcomb 65-ton center-cab switchers were purchased by the U.S military branches in the 1940's for wartime service. The locomotives were of a special lightweight, close-clearance design for use on foreign systems. Like the GE 44-tonners, the Whitcombs were powered by a pair of Caterpillar engines producing 380 h.p. and had a center cab.

Whitcomb began as an independent manufacturer of mining equipment, entered the internal-combustion and electric industrial locomotive market and eventually became part of the Baldwin Locomotive Works. After the war, many Whitcomb military locomotives were sold as surplus and made their way into the used locomotive market where they were found to be an ideal size for industrial uses. Some may have been sold to equipment lessors who leased them to power-short railroads, one of which appears to have been the O&W.

Little is known of the arrangements made by the O&W with a leasing company—reportedly S. M. Healey—or with any defense agency of the federal government, but two—and probably more—Whitcombs, worked on the road in the late 1940's. Several mechanical department bulletins dated March 1947 concerning the operation and maintenance of these locomotives have been found, but they did not specify numbers or

(FACING PAGE) Creating the appearance of a gala event, the presence of the Train of Tomorrow in Middletown brought an air of wonder and anticipation. If the train did in fact arrive from the north, any dome passengers must have instinctively ducked their heads as the cars entered Hawk Mountain, Fallsburg and High View Tunnels. This train was in historical contrast to the anachronistic O&W practice of making meal stops at Middletown station.—W.C. MUELLER COLLECTION.

New Haven 0772 sits in interchange on the O&W at Sidney. NH eventually would acquire 27 PA's, and it's possible that all of them were delivered via the O&W.—CLYDE CONROW COLLECTION.

Like returning servicemen after the war, the military Whitcombs had seen a wider world, and many returned with scars they would carry for the rest of their lives. In this Feb. 1, 1947, scene at Middletown, the 8468 carries the "scars" of buffers on the pilot as well as evidence of other changes that marked the differences between U.S. and foreign railroad practices. The newness of the bolts holding the footboards implies a recent visit to Middletown shops. Two of these units on the O&W were leased from S. M. Healy Co. and were said to be light gray or green with gold lettering. How many of these 65-tonners were on the O&W, who their owners were and how long they were on the property are questions yet to be answered.—JOHN P. AHRENS, COURTESY OF RAY W. BROWN.

What a striking contrast the low-slung, shiny, ACF Talgo Train makes with the grassy tracks and dark bricks of Middletown station. The date is August 1955, and the O&W has not run scheduled passenger service for two years. The train was on its way to the New Haven, whose CEO at the time was the flamboyant Patrick B. McGinnis. In a quest to provide fast, attractive passenger service, he asked ACF and other companies to provide experimental trains which he was eager to bring to the New Haven. The design, in which the railcars are "trailered," with weight-bearing wheelsets at one end only, was based upon trains that were (and still are) very successful in Spain. As this book goes to press in 1994, an updated Talgo design is demonstrating on U.S. rails. It's a curious footnote to realize that O&W played a small part in an innovative rail transportation concept that was still being studied nearly four decades later.
—MARV COHEN.

owners. A dispatchers' train-order book for early September 1949 shows several orders issued to "USA 1368" for movements between Middletown and Summitville and between Monticello and Port Jervis. The 1947 photograph on the previous page shows a unit numbered 8468 and said to be lettered for the Army Transportation Corps. One of these Whitcombs was involved in a serious grade-crossing accident on Route 17 next to the Wurtsboro station. The locomotive was derailed and a truck driver is believed to have been killed.

These diesels show up on the property at the time that the O&W was leasing steam locomotives from the Jersey Central, D&H and New Haven to cope with a postwar boom in freight traffic. At the same time, the railroad wanted to retire as many worn steam locomotives as possible as the reduced costs of diesel operations was most welcome. Until the 1948 order for additional EMD road power and switchers arrived, a variety of steam and diesel locomotives were borrowed to fill in. Once the new power came in, there is no indication that borrowed or leased power remained on the O&W.

ACF's Talgo Train "En Route"

The American Car & Foundry Company (ACF) was a supplier of freight and passenger cars to the industry for many years. At the urging of New Haven President Patrick B. McGinnis, ACF, Pullman-Standard, Budd and locomotive manufacturers Fairbanks-Morse and Baldwin-Lima-Hamilton put together several lightweight, high-speed demonstration trains that were to revolutionize rail passenger service. All

trains proved only marginally successful.

ACF's train was based upon the Talgo design, popularized by the Spanish, with semipermanently coupled aluminum cars behind an 810-h.p. Fairbanks-Morse diesel-electric locomotive. The first train proved rough-riding and noisy. A second demonstrator, shown in the above photograph, was built at ACF's Berwick, Pa., plant.

The new train was completed in 1955 and tested on the Lackawanna before heading for the New Haven. It is likely that the Middletown station picture was taken on the delivery run after Lackawanna handed it over to the O&W. Unfortunately, McGinnis left the New Haven under political storm clouds shortly after the second ACF train arrived. The incoming administration, finding the railroad in deep financial distress, scaled back the lightweight-train program, and the Talgo train never entered regular service.

Erie Power on Detour Trains

The hurricane-created floods of 1955 did minimal damage to the O&W but devastated neighboring roads. Erie was forced to detour over the O&W between Middletown and Sidney for part of that summer, and it was reported that O&W handled some 5,000 additional freight cars during the period. Certainly O&W power alone could not have handled such volume, and Erie power and crews—under the guidance of O&W pilots—got to see new scenery. It was one of those detours, led by Erie F7 712, that was the cause of that penciled notation in an employees' timetable mentioned at the beginning of this chapter.

And it was all a part of the curious diesel doin's on the O&W.

NYO&W Diesel Dispositions

The 44-tonners

101 [GE 15028] and 105 [GE 15032]: Sold to equipment dealer Hyman Michaels in 1951 for $26,000 each, then to Salt Lake, Garfield & Western to become its D.S. 1 and D. S. 2. As of early July 1994, both are still on the property but not in regular service.

102 [GE 15029]: Sold to Mississippi Export Railroad, Moss Point, Miss., for $25,000 in June 1950 and became ME's No. 47. Then sold to the Fernwood, Columbia & Gulf and then to Fort Dodge, Des Moines & Southern where it became No. 502. In 1969 it was believed to have been sold to International Railway Equipment Co. who reportedly has scrapped the unit.

103 [GE 15030]: Sold to the FC&G in August 1950 for $25,000, then sold to the FtDDM&S to become its 503. Then sold in 1969 to International Railway Equipment which stored it at GE's Erie (Pa.) plant and then sold it to Simplot Chemicals Ltd., Brandon, Man., which eventually retired and scrapped it.

104 [GE15031]: Sold in June 1952 to Frank M. Judge, then to Great Northern Paper Co. in Maine circa 1956. Rebuilt by GE later that year and sold through George Silcott to the Hartwell Railway of Hartwell, Ga. Now in possession of Atlanta Chapter-NRHS.

The NW2's

111 [EMD 3164]: Sold to M. S. Kaplan (connected with Salzberg?), then to Unadilla Valley Railway, and then to Chicago, Rock Island & Pacific in March 1959 to become CRI&P 795. Sold to Chrome Crankshaft in February 1981, then to Rail Switching Service, Dothan, Ala., which leased it to International Paper, Atlanta, Texas, where it was in service as of July 1992.

112 [EMD 3165]: Same history as above until becoming CRI&P 796. Chrome Crankshaft says it or Rock Island scrapped the unit, but records not specific.

113 [EMD 3166]: Same history as above up to becoming CRI&P 797; disposition unknown.

114 [EMD 3167]: To NYC in June 1957 as the first of 17 O&W NW2's so disposed and became NYC 9500. Became Penn Central 8683 and then Conrail 9263. Retired on April 11, 1985; scrapped by CR in April 1986.

115 [EMD 3168]: Sold to Northern Pacific in June 1957 (for $64,175) and became NP 2nd 99 then BN 586. Then to Hyman-Michaels, which sold it to Seaboard Allied Milling Co. (SAMX) at Minot, N.D. Through unknown transaction(s), became Cargill 586 in December 1989. [Note 1]

116 [EMD 3169]: Became NYC 9501, PC 8684 and CR 9264 before being retired on Aug. 4, 1986. Purchased by Aldelbert Button (of NYS&W board of directors)

and currently (as of July 1994) operated by New York, Susquehanna & Western.

117 [EMD 3170]: Became NYC 9502, PC 8685 and CR 9265. Retired on Feb. 26, 1981, and sold to Midwest Steel on May 24, 1981.

118 [EMD 3171]: Became NYC 9503, PC 8686. Rebuilt in 1969 to PC 9156. Became CR 9156 and retired on June 6, 1984. Sold to Central Soya in March 1985.

119 [EMD 3172]: Became NYC 9504, PC 8687 and CR 9266. Retired on Aug. 4, 1986, and scrapped by CR.

120 [EMD 3173]: Became NYC 9505, PC 8688. Rebuilt in 1974 to PC 9099. Became CR 9182 and was retired on June 25, 1981. Sold to Midwest Steel.

121 [EMD 3174]: Became NYC 9506, PC 8689 and CR 9267. Retired on June 25, 1981, and sold to Midwest Steel on Jan. 8, 1982.

122 [EMD 3175]: To NYC 9507, PC 8690 and CR 9268. Retired on June 6, 1984, and scrapped Nov. 3, 1984.

123 [EMD 3176]: To NYC 9508, PC 8691 and CR 9269. Retired on Feb. 11, 1981, and traded in to EMD on June 11, 1983, on SD50 order.

124 [EMD 3177]: Became NYC 9509, PC 8692 and CR 9270. Retired on April 14, 1983, and traded in to EMD on June 11, 1983, on SD50 order.

125 [EMD 3178]: Became NYC 9510, PC 8693 and CR 9271. Retired April 11, 1985, and scrapped July 8, 1986.

126 [EMD 3179]: Became NYC 9511, PC 8694 and CR 9272. Retired Nov. 25, 1982, and traded in to EMD on Nov. 28, 1983, on SD50 order.

127 [EMD 3180]: Became NYC 9512, PC 8695. Rebuilt in 1974 to PC 9177. Became CR 9177 and was retired on May 22, 1981, and sold to Midwest Steel(?). Later purchased by George Silcott who sold it to Golden Oak Mining, Isom, Ky., as its No. 2. [Note 2]

128 [EMD 6160]: Became NYC 9513, PC 8696. Rebuilt in 1970 to PC 9101. Became CR 9184; was retired on June 6, 1984, and scrapped on April 15, 1985.

129 [EMD 6161]: Became NYC 9514, PC 8697 and CR 9273. Retired on Feb. 26, 1981, and traded to EMD on June 10, 1983, on SD50 order.

130 [EMD 6162]: Became NYC 9515, PC 8698 and CR 9274. Retired on Feb. 11, 1981. Sold to Midwest Steel [Note 2] on March 25, 1982 (or possibly leased or sold to New England Produce, Boston, Mass., by Oct. 2, 1971). It appears to be now be owned by New Eng-

land Milling Co., Ayer, Mass., and is numbered 1000. [Note 3]

131 [EMD 6163]: Became NYC 9516, PC 8699 and CR 9275. Retired on Feb. 11, 1981, and traded in to EMD on June 11, 1983, on SD50 order.

Notes on NW2 dispositions

1. Cargill does have a lomotive numbered 586, however its serial number does not match that of O&W 115.

2. Midwest Steel was a subsidiary of Diversified Industries Inc., which was liquidated or sold off. Diversified claimed that records of any locomotive transactions cannot be found.

3. New England Produce claims that it did not own CR 9274, nee O&W 130. However New England Milling confirms it has a locomotive numbered 1000.

The FT's

Nos. 601 [EMD 3139-3141], 801 [EMD 3123-3131], 802 [EMD 3124-3132], 803 [EMD 3125-3133], 804 [EMD 3126-3134], 805 [EMD 3127-3135], 806 [EMD 3128-3136], 807 [EMD 3129-3137], 808 [EMD 3130-3138]: Nos. 60l, 801-805, 808 sold to dealer Harold Gottfried in June 1957 for $155,000, for intended resale in Mexico. After years in storage, acquired by NYC for trade-in to EMD and then scrapped by 1968. National Metal & Steel Corporation of Terminal Island, Calif., paid $63,000 for 806 and 807 on June 27, 1957, and sold them to the B&O, where the A units became 4412 and 4413, and the B units 5412 and 5413. Traded in to EMD in 1962.

The F3's

Nos. 501 [EMD 3146], 502 [EMD 3147], 503 [EMD 3148]: The three 500-series F3's were sold in June 1957 to Hyman Michaels, then to Sacramento Northern, a Western Pacific subsidiary. The 501 and 502 became SN 301 and 302, later 301-A and 301-D. Both were retired in May 1971 and traded to EMD that same year. The 503 eventually became WP 801-D, apparently not used by SN but leased to WP in August 1957 and saw occasional use on the famed *California Zephyr* (One source indicates that it was assigned SN number 303 and leased to the WP in November 1957.) It later became WP 926-A and was traded in to EMD in October 1970.

821 [EMD 3142-3144] and 822 [EMD 3143-3145]: The four 800-series F3's were sold to the Erie in June 1957 for general freight service as units 714A, B, C and D. After the Erie Lackawanna merger in 1960, they became EL 7141-7144. Both A units were traded to EMD in 1965. The former 822B was damaged in a wreck at Sterling, Ohio, in 1966, and was scrapped with the 821B that year.

(ABOVE LEFT) Sacramento Northern F3's 301-A&B (ex-O&W 501 and 502) at Sacramento in July 1969.—MIKE SCHAFER.
(ABOVE RIGHT) Salt Lake, Garfield & Western D.S. 2 (nee O&W 105) in 1968.—AUTHOR'S PHOTO.

Bibliography

Books

Bush, Donald J. THE STREAMLINED DECADE. New York: George Braziller, 1975.

Bux, Joe, and Ed Crist. NEW YORK, ONTARIO & WESTERN RAILWAY, SCRANTON DIVISION. Middletown, N.Y.: Ontario & Western Historical Society, 1985.

Carson, Robert B. MAIN LINE TO OBLIVION, THE DISINTEGRATION OF THE NEW YORK RAILROADS IN THE TWENTIETH CENTURY. Port Washington, N.Y.: National University Publications, 1971.

Cray, Ed. CHROME COLOSSUS; GENERAL MOTORS AND ITS TIMES. New York: McGraw-Hill, 1980.

Crist, Ed, and John Krause. O&W: THE FINAL YEARS. Fredon, N.J.: Carstens Publications, 1977.

Del Grosso, Robert C. BURLINGTON NORTHERN 1980-1991 ANNUAL. Denver: Hyrail Productions, 1991.

Diesel Electric Locomotives 1925-1938 from LOCOMOTIVE CYCLOPEDIA. Reprinted in TRAIN SHED CYCLOPEDIA No. 20. Novato, Calif.: Newton K. Gregg, 1974.

———. DIESEL, THE MODERN POWER. Detroit: General Motors Corporation, 1936.

Dolzall, Gary W. and Stephen F. Dolzall. DIESELS FROM EDDYSTONE: THE STORY OF BALDWIN DIESEL LOCOMOTIVES. Milwaukee, Wis.: Kalmbach Publishing, 1984.

Douglas, George H. ALL ABOARD! THE RAILROAD IN AMERICAN LIFE. New York: Paragon House, 1992.

Draney, John. DIESEL LOCOMOTIVES, MECHANICAL EQUIPMENT. Chicago: American Technical Society, 1943.

Farrell, Jack W., and Mike Pearsall. THE MOUNTAINS. Edmonds, Wash.: Pacific Fast Mail, 1977.

Farrington, S. Kip Jr. RAILROADING FROM THE REAR END. New York: Coward, McCann Inc., 1946.

Farrington, S. Kip Jr. RAILROADING THE MODERN WAY, New York: Coward, McCann Inc., 1951.

Hayden, Bob, ed. MODEL RAILROADER CYCLOPEDIA-VOLUME 2: DIESEL LOCOMOTIVES. Milwaukee, Wis.: Kalmbach Publishing, 1980.

Helmer, William F. O&W: THE LONG LIFE AND SLOW DEATH OF THE NEW YORK, ONTARIO & WESTERN RY. Berkley, Calif.: Howell-North, 1959.

Huges, Thomas P. AMERICAN GENESIS. New York: Viking, 1989.

Jones, Jesse H., with Edward Angly. FIFTY BILLION DOLLARS, MY THIRTEEN YEARS WITH THE RFC. New York: Macmillan Co., 1951.

Kasson, John F. CIVILIZING THE MACHINE, TECHNOLOGY AND REPUBLICAN VALUES IN AMERICA. New York: Grossman, 1976.

Kirkland, John F. DAWN OF THE DIESEL AGE. Glendale, Calif.: Interurban Press, 1983.

Kirkland, John F. THE DIESEL BUILDERS, VOLUME ONE, Fairbanks-Morse and Lima-Hamilton. Glendale, Calif.: Interurban Press, 1985.

Kirkland, John F. THE DIESEL BUILDERS, VOLUME TWO, American Locomotive Company and Montreal Locomotive Works. Glendale, Calif.: Interurban Press, 1989.

Lewis, Robert G. HANDBOOK OF AMERICAN RAILROADS. New York: Simmons-Boardman, 1951.

"Locos of the 40's & 50's (Diesel) Part 7" from the 1941 LOCOMOTIVE CYCLOPEDIA AND RAILWAY MECHANICAL ENGINEER. Reprinted in TRAIN SHED CYCLOPEDIA No. 58. Novato, California: Newton K. Gregg, 1977.

"Locos of the 40's & 50's (Diesel) Part 8" from the 1941 LOCOMOTIVE CYCLOPEDIA AND RAILWAY MECHANICAL ENGINEER. Reprinted in TRAIN SHED CYCLOPEDIA No. 60. Novato, California: Newton K. Gregg, 1977.

"Locos of the 40's & 50's (Diesel) Part 11" from the 1941 LOCOMOTIVE CYCLOPEDIA AND RAILWAY MECHANICAL ENGINEER. Reprinted in TRAIN SHED CYCLOPEDIA No. 80. Rohnert Park, Calif.: Newton K. Gregg, 1979.

Marcus, Alan I. and Howard P. Segal. TECHNOLOGY IN AMERICA: A BRIEF HISTORY. New York: Harcourt Brace Jovanovich, 1989.

Martin, Albro. RAILROADS TRIUMPHANT. New York: Oxford University Press, 1992.

McCall, John B. SANTA FE'S EARLY DIESEL DAZE. Dallas, Texas: Kachina Press, 1980.

McGowan, George F. DIESEL-ELECTRIC LOCOMOTIVE HANDBOOK, MECHANICAL EQUIPMENT. New York: Simmons-Boardman, 1951.

Miller, Donald L. and Richard E. Sharpless. E. KINGDOM OF COAL. Philadelphia: University of Pennsylvania Press, 1985.

Morgan, David P. DIESELS WEST! Milwaukee, Wis.: Kalmbach Publishing, 1963.

Morrison. L. H. HIGH SPEED DIESEL ENGINES. Chicago: American Technical Society, 1937.

Mulhearn, Daniel J. and John R. Taibi. GENERAL MOTORS' F-UNITS THE LOCOMOTIVES THAT REVOLUTIONIZED RAILROADING. New York: Quadrant Press, 1982.

Mumford, Lewis. TECHNICS AND CIVILIZATION. New York: Harcourt, Brace and Co., 1934.

Myers, Daniel Frank. THE WOOD CHEMICAL INDUSTRY IN THE DELAWARE VALLEY. Middletown, N.Y.: O&W Historical Society, 1986.

Olson, James Stuart. HERBERT HOOVER AND THE RECONSTRUCTION FINANCE CORPORATION 1931-1933. Ames, Iowa: The Iowa State University Press, 1977.

———. OUR GM SCRAPBOOK. Milwaukee: Kalmbach Publishing Co, 1971.

Pinkepank, Jerry A. DIESEL SPOTTER'S GUIDE. Milwaukee: Kalmbach Publishing, 1967.

Reck, Franklin M. THE DILWORTH STORY. New York: McGraw-Hill Book Co., 1954.

Reck, Franklin M. ON TIME. N.p.: General Motors Corp, 1948.

Reed, Robert C. THE STREAMLINE ERA. San Marino, Calif.: Golden West, 1975.

Rehor, John A. THE NICKEL PLATE STORY. Milwaukee: Kalmbach Publishing, 1965.

Schivelbusch, Wolfgang. THE RAILWAY JOURNEY, THE INDUSTRIALIZATION OF TIME AND SPACE IN THE 19TH CENTURY. Berkley, Calif.: The University of California Press, 1986.

Schrenk, Lorenz P., and Robert L. Frey. NORTHERN PACIFIC DIESEL ERA (1945-1970), Vol. 2. San Marino, Calif.: Golden West Books, 1988.

Sloan, Alfred P. Jr. with Catherine Stevens. MY YEARS WITH GENERAL MOTORS. Ed. John McDonald. Garden City, N.Y.: Doubleday & Co., 1964.

Staff, Virgil. D-DAY ON THE WESTERN PACIFIC. Glendale, Calif.: Interurban Press, 1982.

Stilgoe, John R. Metropolitan Corridor: RAILROADS AND THE AMERICAN SCENE. New Haven, Conn.: Yale University Press, 1983.

Strapac, Joseph A. COTTON BELT LOCOMOTIVES. Huntington Beach, Calif.: Shade Tree Books, 1977.

Strapac, Joseph A. WESTERN PACIFIC'S DIESEL YEARS. Muncie, Ind.: Overland Rail Books, 1980.

Wakefield, Manville B. TO THE MOUNTAINS BY RAIL. Grahamsville, N.Y.: Wakefair Press, 1970.

Weller, John L. THE NEW HAVEN RAILROAD, ITS RISE AND FALL. New York: Hastings House, 1969.

Periodicals

Best, Gerald M. "History and Motive Power of the New York, Ontario & Western Railroad." Railway & Locomotive Historical Society Bulletin No. 40 (May 1936): 16-32.

Bifano, John and Allan Seebach, Ed. "The FT's." Ontario & Western Observer, Vol. 24, Nos. 1-6. (Published by the O&W Railway Historical Society)

Brown, C. A. "Domes On the New Haven." Shoreliner. Vol. 20, No. 1: 32-36.

Cook, Preston. "Electro-Motive's FT Celebrates 50 Years." Railfan & Railroad, October 1989: 46-58.

Cook, Preston. "Electro-Motive's FT Celebrates 50 Years." Railfan & Railroad, November, 1989: 48-55.

Cook, Preston. "Electro-Motive's FT Celebrates 50 Years." Railfan & Railroad, December 1989: 77-80.

"The complex diesel locomotive." Trains. March 1948: 38-39.

Copeland, Alan, and Dan Dover. "GE 44-Tonners." Extra 2200 South. May-June 1975: 14-26.

"Diesel Locomotive Dynamic Brake Expedites Train Operation." Railway Age. Vol. 117, No. 11: 400-402.

Dover, Don. "All about F's." Extra 2200 South. January 1970: 19-21.

Dover, Don. "All About SW's." Extra 2200 South. July-August 1973: 20-24.

Dover, Don. "GE 44-Tonner Study." Extra 2200 South. March-April 1975: 15-25.

"Dual Service Mother Hubbards of the NYO&W". Locomotive Quarterly. Vol. 2, no. 3, (Spring, 1978): 38-63.

"Electro-Motive's F Units." Railroad Model Craftsman. April 1966: 27-31.

"Electro-Motive's F-3." Trains. December 1946: 52-53.

"The Electro-Motive Type F-3 Diesel." Railway Age. Oct. 26, 1946: 674-683.

"E. M. D.'s All-Purpose Diesel." Railway Mechanical Engineer. February 1947: 56-68.

"E-M. D. Diesel Road Locomotives." Railway Mechanical Engineer. May 1949: 247-250.

"Electro-Motive Switchers." Railway Mechanical Engineer. December 1949: 726-730.

"Electro-Motive FT: first freight diesel." Model Railroader. April 1975: 48-51.

"Equipment of the New York, Ontario & Western Railway." Railroad Model Craftsman. March 1963: 20-23.

Frattasio, Mark and Joel Rosenbaum. "The McGinnis Trains—Chapter 1." Shoreliner. Vol. 19, No. 2: 10-38.

Frattasio, Mark and Joel Rosenbaum. "The McGinnis Trains—Chapter 4." Shoreliner. Vol. 20, No. 4: 8-29.

"From coal road to bridge route." Trains. August, 1949: 36-37.

"GE 44-ton switcher." Model Railroader. April 1973: 50-51.

Gillilan, P. M. "Diesel-Electric Locomotive for Light Service." Railway Age. Nov. 23, 1940: 784-786.

Gross, H. H. "Shawangunk Barrier." Railroad Magazine. September 1946: 11-43.

Hahn, Jr., John D. "Last Days of the O&W." Diesel Era. November/December 1992: 8-13 +.

Hamilton, H. L. "Diesel Engine Development & Application to Mobile Equipment in America." Published by The Newcomen Society of the United States, 1944. (Address, given in Chicago, before The Newcomen Society of England on Nov. 18, 1942.)

Hanlon, Larry, and Peter Solyom, Ed. "WP FT's." The Headlight, issue No. 7, Vol. 92, No. 1. (Published by the Feather River Rail Society and the Western Pacific Railroad Historical Society. Entire issue is devoted the history of the Western Pacific's FT's.)

"How a diesel works." Trains. October, 1952: 28-29.

"How the Diesel Locomotive Works." Railroad Magazine. May 1943: 78-87.

Iczkowski, Mike. "Daybreak at LaGrange." Trains. August 1976: 29-31.

Klein, Maury. "The Diesel Revolution." American Heritage of Invention &Technology. Winter 1991: 16-22.

Kreitner, Ken. "Lament for an Old Woman." Trains. February 1981: 31-32.

Lampert, A. A. "A 44-Tonner Turns in Work Report." Railway Age. Oct. 9, 1943.

"Locomotive Roster of the New York, Ontario & Western." Railroad Magazine. May 1943: 105-109.

Malinoski, Robert R. "NYO&W Scranton Division: March 17, 1933." Trains. March, 1987: 44-50.

Marre, Louis A. "F-3." Railroad Model Craftsman. August 1970: 19-25.

Mehndar, J. "NYO&W's orphan F's." Pacific News. February 1975: 3.

"The Mighty O&W." Courier Magazine. October 1953: 7-10 +.

"Model F-3 A and B Units." Model Railroader. (Reprint, Kalmbach Publishing Co.) 1949.

"Model FT A and B Units." Model Railroader. (Reprint, Kalmbach Publishing Co.) 1949.

Mohowski, Robert E. "O&W 116: The Comeback Kid." Railpace Newsmagazine. June 1987: 32-35.

Morgan, David P. "Can steam locomotives be standardized?" Trains. December 1947: 42-44.

Morgan, David P. "The diesel that did it." Trains. January 1960:18-25.

Morgan, David P. "Diesel vs. Diesel." Trains. September 1949: 14-17.

Morgan, David P. "Electro-Motive: young giant." Trains. November 1948: 46-51.

Morgan, David P. "Farewell to the FT." Trains. March, 1962: 42-47.

Morgan, David P. "He sold streamlining." Trains. July 1952: 12-17.

Morgan, David P. "It's dungarees for the diesel." Trains. May 1953: 50-57.

Morgan, David P. "We're not a foundry any more!" Trains. July, 1954: 23-30.

Moyers, Jerry T. "The Alco RS1: Grandaddy of the road switchers." Railroad Model Craftsman. May, 1991: 60-66.

Neusser, A. V. and C. E. Pearce. "The NYO&W." Trains. August, 1942: 20-30.

"New York, Ontario & Western E-Class 4-6-0's." Locomotive Quarterly. Winter, 1989: 38-57.

"New York, Ontario & Western 4-8-2 Types." Locomotive Quarterly. Fall 1991: 42-57.

"Obituary of an Old Woman." Trains. July 1957: 23-30.

"Ontario & Western Sold by Segments." Short-Line Railroader. Summer 1957: 3-5 +.

Roe, Wellington. "Diesels Down East." Railroad Magazine. July 1945: 46-51.

Pennypacker, Bert. "The Diesel That Could Not Replace a Steamer." Trains. May, 1975: 40-47.

Pinkepank, Jerry A. "Everyman's diesel primer." Trains. December 1970: 18-23.

"Santa Fe Installs High-Capacity Diesel-Freight Locomotive." Railway Mechanical Engineer. April, 1941: 133-140.

Roehm, Peter. "The Old Woman of the Shawangunks, The N.Y.O. & W. Story." Jersey Central Lines (Part 1), May 1981: 15-26.

Roehm, Peter. "The Old Woman of the Shawangunks, The N.Y.O. & W. Story." Jersey Central Lines (Part 2), June 1981: 29-39.

"Saga of the 405." Locomotive Quarterly. Fall 1991: 58-61.

Shaughnessy, Jim. "The Diesels that tamed Hoosac." Railfan & Railroad. December 1989: 58-65.

Short-Line Railroader, No. 33. Summer 1957: Ed. Wm. S. Young. Published at Cranford, N.J.

Smith, Vernon L. "The Diesel from D to L - 1." Trains. April 1979: 22-29.

Smith, Vernon L. "The Diesel from D to L - 2." Trains. May 1979: 44-51.

Smith, Vernon L. "The Diesel from D to L - 3." Trains. June 1979: 46-51.

Smith, Vernon L. "The Diesel from D to L - 4." Trains. July 1979: 44-49.

"What is an equipment trust?" Trains. August 1949: 45

Zimmermann, Karl. "40 Years of Domes/Part 1." Passenger Train Journal. December 1985: 13-24.

Other Sources

Darlington, James William. "A Railroad Geography: The New York, Ontario & Western Railway." M.A. Diss., Wilkes College, 1970.

Freeman, Lewis D. "Report On Diesel Locomotive Tests," n.d., n.p. (printed by RFC)

Mohowski, Robert E. "Milk Cans, Mountains, Mixed-Trains, and Motor Cars; The New York, Ontario & Western in Central New York." book manuscript awaiting publication, 1994.

Pratt, George William. "History of the New York, Ontario & Western Railroad." M.A. Diss., Cornell University, 1942.

Slawson, George C. "New York & Oswego Midland Railroad." Manuscript, 1942.

Stellwagen, John C. "The New York & Oswego Midland Railroad Company: The Planning Stages." Manuscript, n.d.

Wm. Wyer & Co. "Report on New York, Ontario & Western Railway Company," prepared for Samuel M. Pinsly.

Annual Reports, New York, Ontario & Western Railway; 1880-1953

N.Y.O. & W. Ry. Co., Reorganization Proceedings in the United States District Court for the Southern District of New York. Vols. 1-24.

Electro Motive Division report: "Application of Diesel Motive-Power on the New York, Ontario & Western Railway Co."

Operating and maintenance manuals, catalogs and sales promotions and literature from General Motors and General Electric

And, several hundred letters, memos, reports, clippings, and bulletins in the collections of Marv Cohen, the O&W Historical Society and others listed in the acknowledgements as well as from those who choose to remain anonymous.